DATE DUE

FRANCO

MILITARY PROFILES
SERIES EDITOR
Dennis E. Showalter, Ph.D.
The Colorado College

*Instructive summaries for general and expert
readers alike, volumes in the Military Profiles
series are essential treatments of significant and
popular military figures drawn from world history,
ancient times through the present.*

FRANCO

MILITARY PROFILES
SERIES EDITOR
Dennis E. Showalter, Ph.D.
The Colorado College

*Instructive summaries for general and expert
readers alike, volumes in the Military Profiles
series are essential treatments of significant and
popular military figures drawn from world history,
ancient times through the present.*

FRANCO

Soldier, Commander, Dictator

Geoffrey Jensen

Potomac Books, Inc.
Washington, D.C.

Library of Congress Cataloging-in-Publication Data

Jensen, Geoffrey, 1965–
    Franco : soldier, commander, dictator / Geoffrey
Jensen.—1st ed.
        p. cm. — (Military profiles)
    Includes bibliographical references and index.
    ISBN 1–57488–644–4 (hardcover : alk. paper)— ISBN
1–57488–645–2 (pbk. : alk. paper)
    1. Franco, Francisco, 1892–1975. 2. Heads of state—
Spain—Biography.   3. Generals—Spain—Biography.
I. Title.   II. Series.

DP264.F7J46   2005
946.082'092—dc22   2005006096

Potomac Books, Inc.
22841 Quicksilver Drive
Dulles, Virginia 20166

FIRST EDITION

10 9 8 7 6 5 4 3 2 1

For Marina

Contents

Contents

List of Maps

Preface

In many ways, Francisco Franco was always a soldier. He grew up in a military family, attended a naval prep school, and donned his first official army uniform at age fourteen, when he entered the Spanish infantry academy. He continued to appear in military dress until his death in 1975, which marked the end of one of the longest and most stable dictatorships in modern history—one that outlasted those of Hitler and Mussolini by decades. Throughout his life, Franco's status as a soldier never ceased to shape his thoughts and actions.

But what does it really mean to be a professional soldier? On the most basic level, it simply means pursuing a career in the army. Although strictly speaking an officer differs from a common soldier, the term "soldier" is often used to describe both. More concretely, the word suggests someone who will take up arms, kill, and possibly die on behalf of his or her country—not just a member of an army's supporting staff.

Soldier has other implications as well. The word usually brings to mind a conservative and authority-minded figure, in personal as well as political spheres. Thus the basic military values of order, hierarchy, and strong rule characterize the stereotypical soldier at home, on the battlefield, and in the world of politics. Moreover, the figure of the career soldier or officer is usually assumed to be male—at least until very recently. For this reason, the expression "military man" is commonplace but "military woman" sounds odd.

Franco, who rose from his professional origins as a small, quiet fourteen-year-old cadet to become one of the twentieth century's longest ruling dictators, was a prototypical soldier. This book, in turn, is a military biography, and it works from the assumption that Franco's condition as a career army officer explains much about his life on and off the battlefield. Franco virtually always acted as a professional soldier, even in non-military situations.

This book is also a military biography in the traditional sense: it examines and interprets Franco's performance as an army officer. One of its principal arguments concerns his understanding of what strategists today call the "operational level of war." This term refers to the area of military thought that falls between and links together strategy and tactics, often stressing ground-air coordination. Franco may not have been a strategic genius, but he grasped the importance of the operational level of war very early, at a time when military technology made rapid advances.

In no small part because of his experiences in combined arms and joint force operations in Morocco, he displayed an unusual appreciation for the need to transcend traditional rivalries and promote intimate cooperation between artillery, air, infantry, and naval units. Franco himself was not always the best person to direct every aspect of these operations, but as a wartime commander in chief, he always made it a priority to staff the relevant positions with officers skilled at operational-level planning, including many not from the infantry.

This book is about more than Franco's military thought, however; it also aims to interest readers to whom traditional battlefield history has little appeal. Indeed, Franco's military actions are not just important in their own right; they also help us to understand his subsequent behavior as dictator and his political, social, and personal views in general. Hitler, Mussolini, and Stalin may have claimed military rank and led their countries' armed forces in war and peace, but none was as much a product of military culture as Francisco Franco.

This book benefited from the assistance of many people. Stanley G. Payne and Kenneth W. Estes read the whole manuscript and provided especially valuable criticism and suggestions. I am also grateful for the willingness of José Álvarez, Jorge Aspizua, Wayne Bowen, Daniel Kowalsky, and Sasha David Pack to read and comment on early versions of chapters. In addition, I wish to give special thanks to the head of the History Department at the University of Southern Mississippi, Charles Bolton. At the Virginia Military Institute, Dean of Faculty Charles F. Brower and History Department head Turk McCleskey have been very supportive of my work. Paul Merzlak, formerly of Brassey's, Inc., also provided me with ample assistance, even if the final responsibility for the book's contents must lie with me alone. Finally, I wish to express immeasurable gratitude to my parents and sisters, whose unconditional love I will always treasure, and to Marina Cabada del Río, to whom I dedicate this book with so much love and affection.

Chronology

1892	Born 4 December in El Ferrol, Galicia, in Northwest Spain.
1898	Spain suffers humiliating military defeat by the United States, thereby losing the last remnants of its overseas empire.
1907	Franco begins his studies at the Infantry Academy in Toledo.
1909	Large-scale ambush of Spanish forces at Wolf Ravine, Morocco. A call-up of reserves sparks the Tragic Week of antiwar and anticlerical rioting in Barcelona.
1910	Franco graduates from the Infantry Academy and is commissioned as a second lieutenant in July.
1912	Posted to Morocco, where he enters into combat for the first time; promotion to first lieutenant.
1913	Spanish forces occupy Tetuan. Franco posted with the *Regulares.*
1916	Franco nearly dies after taking a bullet in the stomach in a battle near the village of El Biutz, Morocco.
1917	Takes part in operations against strikers in Asturias.
1920	Returns to Morocco and becomes the second in command of the newly formed Spanish Foreign Legion in May.
1923	In September Gen. Miguel Primo de Rivera stages a coup and establishes a dictatorship. Franco marries Carmen Polo Martínez Valdés in Oviedo, Asturias, on 22 October.

1925   Franco participates in a large-scale amphibious operation at Al Hoceima Bay.

1926   Promoted to brigadier general; birth of his only child, Carmen Franco Polo (Carmencita).

1928   Franco is appointed head of the newly reestablished *Academia General Militar*.

1931   Proclamation of Spain's first democracy, the Second Republic, on 14 April. Republican War Minister Manuel Azaña announces his decision to close the *Academia General Militar*.

1934   Promoted to major general; coordinates military suppression of the revolutionary insurrection in Asturias.

1936   Franco joins other leading military figures in the uprising against the Second Republic that sparks the Spanish Civil War on 17-18 July. In late September the Nationalists lift the siege of the Alcázar in Toledo.

1937   Battle of Jarama Valley, February. Battle of Guadalajara, March. Guernica bombed by German and Italian planes, April. Battle of Brunete, July.

1938   Battle of the Ebro, July-November.

1939   Franco declares victory in the civil war on 1 April.

1940   Franco meets with Hitler in Hendaye, France, in October.

1943   Seven of Franco's twelve lieutenant generals sign a letter calling for the reestablishment of the monarchy in Spain.

1953   Treaty with the United States allowing for a major U.S. military presence in Spain signed.

1955   Spain admitted to the United Nations.

1956   Morocco gains independence.

1957   War of Ifni (November–February, 1958).

1958   Franco agrees to cede Cabo Juby to Morocco.

1968   In its first killing, the Basque separatist group ETA assassinates the head of the political police in Guipúzcoa. Equatorial Guinea gains independence from Spain.

1970   Burgos trial.

1973   Adm. Luis Carrero Blanco, Franco's most intimate and faithful collaborator, is killed by ETA terrorists in December.

1975   Franco approves the execution of five ETA members on trial for terrorism, commuting the sentences of six others, September. The Green March, 6 November, results in Spain's announcement one week later that it will withdraw from the Sahara. Franco dies 20 November. Juan Carlos then proclaimed king of Spain.

FRANCO

Chapter 1

From Navy Brat to Army Cadet

NOTHING IN FRANCO'S FAMILY background or the first years of his life gave any indication that he would one day determine the fate of so many lives. Born on 4 December 1892 to a family with a tradition of staff service in the Spanish navy, Franco grew up in the Galicia region of northwest Spain, in the small, Atlantic port town of El Ferrol. Galicia bears little semblance to the stereotypical, hot and dry lands of Don Quixote's central Spain. Nor does it resemble the romantic vision of the Mediterranean coast and the flamenco music, gypsies, and bullfights that supposedly characterize life there. In some ways similar to the Pacific Northwest of the United States, Galicia is a very green, rainy, and often cool and damp region. The stereotypical Galician man has little of the bravado and exaggerated personal pride often associated with Spaniards. Instead he is melancholic, soft-spoken, suspicious, and prudent. In fact, to this day Spaniards often argue that Franco's Galician characteristics profoundly shaped his actions as soldier and statesman.[1]

El Ferrol was the principal Atlantic base for the Spanish navy, and Franco's father and grandfather both eventually became

Intendents in its administrative wing, at ranks roughly equivalent to brigadier general in the army. But the relative professional success of Franco's father Nicolás did not bring with it an especially happy family life. Franco and his three siblings—a fourth died in early childhood—grew up as the products of an ultimately failed marriage. Their father had the reputation of someone who enjoyed late nights of drinking and womanizing, and at home he was a strict and bad-tempered man who could turn violent at times. In 1907, the same year Franco entered the Infantry Academy, his father abandoned his family for good, moving in with a servant girl with whom he spent the rest of his life.

Nevertheless, Franco's childhood was not entirely unpleasant, and the Franco children learned to weather the domestic storms in which they grew up fairly well. Their mother, Pilar Bahamonde, was very loving and supporting of her children, and she seems to have imbued Franco and his sister Pilar, in particular, with her belief in turning to hard work and dedication to get through difficult times. This attitude helped Franco to endure his trying times as a cadet after he left home. Franco's mother was also a very religious woman, and he himself displayed the same strongly Catholic-conservative values later in life.

The beliefs of his father, however, were very different. The elder Franco had no interest in religion, rejected many conventional moral values, and held relatively leftist political views in general. He stood, in other words, for all that Franco disliked and sought to combat later in life. Franco's brothers, in contrast, came to resemble their father to a greater degree, although none seems to have had strong feelings of affection for him either. In fact, when their mother died in 1934, all the Franco children tried to ignore their father as best they could when making the funeral arrangements. By this point, his sons, all ambitious, had found success in their own ways.

According to sister Pilar, the oldest brother, Nicolás, suffered the most as a child from his father's fits of anger, but was nevertheless his favorite. When he grew older, Nicolás managed to pursue a noteworthy naval career at a time when the profession was especially competitive. After he resigned from the navy at age thirty-five, he took over as director of a commercial naval shipyard in Valencia, on Spain's Mediterranean coast. He had the reputation of a fun-loving man who liked the nightlife.

The younger brother, Ramón, found much fame as the Spanish version of Charles Lindbergh. In 1926 he made the first transatlantic crossing to Buenos Aires as the senior pilot of the *Plus Ultra*, thereby earning a place in aviation history. In a newspaper interview shortly after the record-setting flight, his father identified Ramón as the most intelligent of his children. Like many pilots at a time when flying was a highly dangerous and often deadly pursuit, he sought to push things to the limit not just in the air, but in the political world as well. By the late 1920s he had embraced radical left-wing politics, and he actively conspired to overthrow the Spanish monarchy and establish a republican government. Three months after the civil war broke out, however, Ramón turned away from his radical past to side with his brother Francisco and the other conservative generals who wanted to overthrow Spain's first democracy. He died during the war in a flying accident.

As children, though, Franco and his brothers had grown up in a home environment that was far from ideal, even if the young Francisco could always turn to his mother for love and emotional support. To make matters worse, the more general background to Franco's childhood was unfortunate as well. The Spanish empire of the 1890s was in serious decline, as the Francos and other Spanish families with strong naval ties were painfully aware.

On the international scene, the once global Spanish empire—extending over multiple continents at its height—had been reduced to Cuba, Puerto Rico, and the Philippines. And this empire disappeared altogether in 1898, when the United States defeated Spain in a war that marked the beginnings of America's own rise as an imperial power. As a boy in the naval town of El Ferrol, Franco was well aware of the consequences of the Spanish empire's decline, and he undoubtedly heard at least some of the arguments that raged in his country over whom or what to blame for the disaster. Although it is doubtful that he had much of a political consciousness at this time, he probably heard the argument that a conspiracy of Freemasons had helped facilitate the Spanish loss of empire. In any case, later in life he did not hesitate to blame Freemasonry for Spain's colonial setbacks and for many other supposed evils of the modern age. On a personal level, the ramifications of 1898 were more immediate. His boyhood companion Camilo Alonso Vega, one of his few life-long friends, lost his father in a naval battle near Cuba.

Moreover, the Spanish defeat of 1898 contributed to the decision by the bankrupt central government to suspend admissions to the Naval Academy in 1907, which meant Franco could not follow professionally in his father's footsteps. In fact, in Franco's mind the 1898 disaster was closely related to his personal fate, and the supposed role Freemasons had played in the military defeat only fueled his life-long fear of Masonic conspiracies. With the navy no longer a possibility even for a naval preparatory school student like himself, Franco decided to turn to the army.

He now had to decide whether to begin his studies at the army's infantry, cavalry, artillery, or engineering academies. The latter two required five years of study at the academy and had the most difficult admissions standards, although they also rewarded graduates with engineering degrees valid in the civilian world along with their commissions as lieutenants. The infantry and cavalry academies, on the other hand, only demanded three years of study, to be followed by two years of practical experience as second lieutenants in an assigned regiment. They were also the easiest in which to gain admission, making them more attainable for someone like Franco, who had no special academic abilities. Franco chose the Infantry Academy in Toledo, which was more open than the cavalry to applicants without family connections.[2]

In August 1907 the small, quiet fourteen-year-old Franco thus entered the Infantry Academy in Toledo. There he was immediately confronted by physical reminders of past imperial greatness that far exceeded anything he had seen in El Ferrol. These reminders helped instill him and the other cadets with strong nationalist values, although they may have also invited unfortunate comparisons between a glorious history and Spain's far from ideal state of affairs at the early twentieth century.

The Infantry Academy was housed in the Alcázar, an enormous, majestic fortress perched spectacularly on a cliff at the edge of the medieval city of Toledo. Its architectural splendor served as a constant reminder to cadets of their great predecessors, although they now had to make due with inadequate and outdated weapons, equipment, and educational methods. Franco seems to have been receptive to exhortations by one of his professors, who urged cadets to "think each day about what the patio arches of the barracks represent, about the bronze inscriptions that adorn the walls, about the past glory once present in the very rooms in which you now walk." The professor implored his young listeners to "capture the spirit and let it take you through history, revering and admiring those who in this very Alcázar earned worldwide respect."[3]

Franco later claimed that his first impression of the academy not only infused him with a strong sense of nationalist historical values, but also caused him to embrace the army wholeheartedly, extinguishing his once-strong desires for the naval life embodied by his hometown and family. He was especially moved by the Alcázar's "entrance and the magnificence of its courtyard of arms, presided over by the statue of Charles V." Tellingly, the inscription at the base of the statue quoted the late emperor's words about a coming campaign in North Africa, the same part of the world where Franco first found his fame: "I will either die in Africa or enter victoriously in Tunis." The overall effect, Franco said, was an indescribable flood of emotion.

Much has been written about Franco's years in the academy, where his particularly small size and rather meek and high-pitched voice did not make life particularly easy. The initial experiences, moreover, were especially difficult for the fourteen-year-old entering cadet, who suffered under initiation rites meted out by the upperclassmen. Life could be difficult for all of the new cadets, but it was especially traumatic for the boy everyone called *Franquito* (little Franco). As an old man, Franco still remembered painfully the initiation rites he had suffered. He also had few close friends at the academy.[4]

But academy life did help prepare him to face the subsequent rigors of military life and the loneliness of command with a noteworthy stoicism, reinforcing his military values and way of looking at life. Years later, when Franco headed the newly reestablished, multi-service General Military Academy, he did his best to draw upon the lessons he had taken from his time as a cadet. And as commander of the rebel forces in the Spanish Civil War and then dictator of his country, he often displayed the same aloof, harsh, and cold personality that seems to have formed in no small part during his difficult days as a cadet.

Militarily speaking, the education and training Franco received in Toledo was common. All arms and branches of service stress their own importance, and the Spanish infantry was certainly no exception. But in early twentieth-century Spain the influence of the infantry within the army as a whole was especially great, even as new technology increasingly favored artillery, engineering, and logistics. To some degree Spanish military leaders had little choice in the matter: the country simply could not afford many modern weapons or other fruits of new technology. Under such conditions it made sense to emphasize the role of the infantry in battle.

On a practical level, the tactical principles Franco learned at the academy were very traditional and did not prove particularly useful when he first saw combat in Morocco. As to be expected, the standard Spanish manual in tactics was aimed at low-level officers and stressed small unit tactics, ignoring the operational and strategic questions that advancing officers presumably learned later at Staff College. But even at the tactical level, the manual had surprisingly little to say about the kind of warfare the cadets would soon face in North Africa. Spain is, of course, the country that gave birth to the military term *guerrilla* for the irregular warriors who had used unconventional methods of terror, hidden attacks, sharpshooting, and independent actions in their struggle against Napoleon's armies. But according to the manual's definition, the term simply meant "a line of men separated between themselves by more or less large intervals" who acted as skirmishers at the head of echelons.[5]

In other words, the manual described guerrillas as a component of traditional, regular-warfare military units: they were the men in the first line of fire of an advancing unit, who would advance in line but then fall into a "guerrilla" formation as they approached the enemy. But Franco and his fellow cadets soon faced an enemy in North Africa who used guerrilla tactics as a method of insurgency and irregular warfare. It is difficult to see, then, how the manual's tactical recommendations—or its general emphasis on regular warfare—could have proved very helpful.

More useful to the cadets would have been manuals explaining that their Moroccan enemies did not follow the traditional rules of European warfare, and that even acting in small numbers they could have deadly consequences for the Spanish occupiers. Although such discussions did take place in some Spanish military books and journals, Franco had little or no exposure to them in his formal readings as a cadet. In fact, years later Franco himself wrote of the irrelevance of the older tactics to the Moroccan campaigns. He even specifically criticized the outdated idea of guerrilla formations that he had learned as a cadet, writing that the old-style formations did little more than create "highly-desired targets" for enemy fire.[6]

Nevertheless, Franco's military education in Toledo was not entirely outmoded and inadequate. Nor was all Spanish military doctrine hopelessly behind the times. Admittedly, infantry cadets learned little in their formal texts about the irregular warfare they confronted in Morocco. It is also true that the official tactical manual recommended leading small-unit attacks against fortified positions using frontal assaults in strict formations, as one biographer of Franco writes. By the early twentieth century such an unimaginative method was often extremely deadly and ultimately unsuccessful against any reasonable amount of firepower. The manual also had little to say about the use of machine guns and other automatic weapons, as critics have noted.[7] But this omission was only part of the story.

In fact, the manual was soon supplemented by a 150-page text devoted solely to the infantry's use of machine guns, and texts on many other aspects of infantry fighting were also published. Some of these manuals discussed surprisingly advanced tactical concepts. For example, several years after Franco received his first commission—but before the British experience at Gallipoli—an official manual on combined infantry and naval tactics in amphibious landings saw print.[8] This manual represented an early step toward the successful Spanish landing at Al Hoceima Bay in 1925, in which Franco took part. The Al Hoceima operation, involving ground, air, and naval forces from two European countries and indigenous North African units, foreshadowed the kind of combined-arms coordination that Franco's side came closest to mastering in the Spanish Civil War.

Franco, then, may not have received the best training and education possible during his stay at the Infantry Academy in Toledo. Many of his professors were not particularly competent.[9] And in any case, he was certainly not an outstanding student; throughout his life, his writings betrayed the lack of a good academic foundation. But this does not mean that his generation of Toledo-educated military elite was always lacking as a whole. Its members overcame initial, grave setbacks in North Africa and eventually developed the tactical and operational methods that finally achieved control of the occupied territories, albeit at a very high cost to Moroccans and Spaniards alike. The director of studies and later overall director of the academy was Col. José Villalba Riquelme, a man who spent much of his career in North Africa and whose path soon crossed Franco's again.

Another frequent criticism of Franco's military education concerns its outdated emphasis on traditional infantry tactics rather than the modern use of artillery and other technological advances in weapons and equipment. Indeed, many of his professors clearly did stress the moral forces in warfare, including a fighting spirit, nationalist fervor, and morale, instead of new technology. The implication to cadets—sometimes made explicitly—was that such moral attributes could make it possible to overcome an enemy with superior weapons but an insufficient fighting spirit.

For this reason, the Russo-Japanese War of 1904–5 generated intense discussion in some military circles. In this war the Japanese had seemingly used their superior spirit of nationalist self-sacrifice and warrior values to overcome the defensive firepower of their Russian opponents. The war had made an especially strong impression on military thinkers all over Europe, in part for racist reasons: most had not expected the non-white, Japanese armed forces to defeat a European army like that of the Russians.

Franco's dictatorship later promoted the supposed lessons of the war and of the Japanese warrior ethos Bushido. During his days as a cadet, Franco probably did not pay much direct attention to the supposed morals of the Russo-Japanese War, but the conflict influenced what he was taught. Thereafter, the lessons of the war reached him and other key officers explicitly while they were serving in Morocco. José Millán-Astray, the founder of the Spanish Foreign Legion under whom Franco served in the 1920s, deemed the subject highly relevant to Spain; more than a decade earlier he had made lessons in Bushido a part of the curriculum in his class on "military morals" at the Infantry Academy. The appeal of emphasizing spiritual, moral forces and warrior values—like those of Bushido—over modern weapons and technology was especially strong in a country like Spain, which could not afford to modernize its war-fighting capabilities even if it so desired.

Yet it is important to remember that Franco and other Spanish officers-to-be were not the only European cadets to receive a military education emphasizing infantry morale and the supposed superiority of an inspired frontal attack over defensive firepower and technology. In fact, armies throughout the Western world had not only drawn the same lessons as the Spaniards from the Russo-Japanese War, but they had interpreted them as further support for doctrines advocating direct attacks against fortified positions. This so-called cult of the offensive characterized much military doctrine until at least the first part of World War I, even in those countries with far more money than Spain to spend on new artillery and other more advanced technological alternatives to the old-fashioned, morale-driven infantry attack.

In a sense, moreover, the Spanish advocates of the cult of the offensive had more justification for their emphasis on morale than did their counterparts from the richer and better-equipped armies of Germany and France, especially before the bloodbaths of World War I made the dangers of frontal attack painfully apparent. With such poor material resources, the Spaniards had no other option. The Infantry Academy in Toledo may have failed to incorporate all the lessons of modern warfare and technology into its curriculum, but this failure did not necessarily indicate that Spanish military doctrine was hopelessly behind the times.[10]

Furthermore, the Spanish Infantry Academy was not the only such institution in Europe to teach ostensibly outdated skills, and many academies continue to do so to this day. In many cases the goal is not so much technical or practical as it is the imparting of collective military values. Such an aim can serve as justification for the continued presence of everything from the many stables at Britain's Royal Academy Sandhurst to the courses on sailing and traditional seamanship at the U.S. Naval Academy. And this aim largely explains the countless hours of drilling on paved surfaces that cadets everywhere still must endure—even in an age of mass motorized transport and rapid loading and firing weapons.

Admittedly, politics and special interests had an especially strong tendency in Spain to hinder the translation of ideas into practice. Indeed, the Spanish military suffered from an acute professional-bureaucratic culture of resistance to change. Hence, the obstacles that would-be reformers faced were often the making of military officers themselves and their own political and corporate interests.[11]

Nevertheless, the graduates of the Infantry Academy from Franco's generation entered the Spanish military world at a time when—at least at the theoretical level—its elite were particularly diverse and receptive to new ideas and debates. The graduates may not have absorbed much, if any, of this intellectual dynamism as cadets, but the more intelligent and interested ones could later do so through Spain's many journals of military thought, public presentations, and staff colleges. Franco himself—who graduated only 251st in an academy class of 312 cadets—never excelled in this world, and he barely participated in the thriving elite Spanish military culture of books, periodicals, and intellectual societies.

He did, however, eventually reap the benefits of some of the better operational thinkers to come out of this culture, bringing together their talents with the practical leadership skills he acquired in Morocco. The final ingredients in this effective mixture were luck and the set of military and conservative nationalist values that his Toledo education had so deeply ingrained in his psyche. In the end, he learned to harness and steer these elements, took advantage of the right domestic and international conditions, and emerged as a triumphant commander in chief and long-ruling dictator.

Chapter 2

Blood and Glory in Morocco

F RANCO GRADUATED from the Infantry Academy
and received his commission as a second lieutenant in July 1910.
Nobody forecast then that ninety-six of his classmates would
lose their lives in Morocco or the Spanish Civil War. Nor did
anyone forecast that almost 1,000 Spanish officers and 16,000 of
their soldiers would meet their deaths in North Africa during
Franco's time there. But even if Franco had fully realized the
extent of the dangers, the ambitious young man would have requested a Moroccan assignment. Much to his dismay, however,
he was sent first to the Eighth Zamora Regiment, headquartered
in his hometown of El Ferrol. He waited a year and a half to set
foot in North Africa.[1]

In February 1912 the nineteen-year-old Franco received his
orders to report to the captain-general (military governor) of
Melilla, a North African city that, along with its counterpart to
the west, Ceuta, still belongs to Spain. Spain had acquired the
two cities centuries before, and they remain Spanish to this
day—much as Gibraltar on the southern Spanish coast is still in
British hands. As Franco was well aware, the situation in North

Africa had been heating up for several years, and Spanish business, political, and military interests there now met increasing resistance.

Morocco was a country characterized by much diversity and armed rivalries between different tribes and warlords. A monarchy served to unify the country, with its Muslim majority and significant Jewish minority. But to European eyes it lacked the kind of strong central government that all modern states need, and suffered under an increasingly week sultanate. According to the rather self-serving reasoning of the Europeans, this chaotic land of multiple ethnic groups, languages, and rulers needed outside intervention to restore order. During the nineteenth century, moreover, business interests combined with the pressures of nationalist imperialism and Europe's "scramble for Africa" to strengthen the Spanish colonialist argument even further.

Spain did not wish to be left out. Indeed, many Spaniards believed that they were most suited of all the western powers to intervene in Morocco, a country so close that they could see it with the naked eye across the seven-mile strait flowing between Spain and Africa. In addition to this geographical link, they maintained, Spain and Morocco share unique historic, cultural, and ethnic ties. After the imperial losses of 1898, pressures to expand in Morocco came from segments of the Spanish military as well, which had no other avenue for the exciting and professionally advantageous combat that some officers so desperately wanted.

The modern era of Spanish military operations in Morocco began in 1859, when Spanish troops put down a revolt by area tribesmen in a six-month campaign. The campaign yielded a series of Spanish military victories, although it caused around 7,000 deaths. In addition, it inspired some sectors of Spanish society to call for further expansion in North Africa.[2] These voices were not, however, unanimous, and the long and bloody experience in Morocco provoked even more intense divisions, political turmoil, and social strife back home on the Spanish peninsula than the war in Vietnam caused on the U. S. home front.

For Franco, Morocco had first become a serious concern during the summer before his final year as a cadet in Toledo. The problem involved Spanish troops stationed in Melilla, about 155 nautical miles east of Ceuta. Melilla is on the northeastern coast of the Moroccan Rif, a region centered on a mountainous range extending about 180 miles in a horizontal strip just south of the Mediterranean. It is an area of geographic extremes, and Spanish forces found their operations there especially difficult.

The western extension of the Rif mountains, with their valleys, forested slopes, and mountain heights of up to 8,000 feet, receive ample rainfall that blows in from the sea to the west. To the east the mountains tower to equally impressive heights, forming the central Rif range. In the west and to the south the heavy winter rainfall combines with melting snow to fill rushing rivers and streams, while the region becomes drier to the east. Although the Rif lacks large rivers, some of the many streams run through deep gullies and ravines, creating compartments that made things very difficult for the Spaniards. In the eastern region the Spanish army had to operate in temperatures that could fall well below freezing even in the valleys, while in the summer they suffered from horrible heat.

The Berber tribes who inhabit the Rif were known for their strong spirit of independence, which they made deadly clear to the Spanish occupiers. Even before colonization by Europeans, the Moroccan government could not always control the area. In fact, a 1799 treaty between Spain and Morocco did not apply to the Rif coast because there was no way to prevent locals from attacking Spanish ships. In more recent times, Rifians have continued to reveal a strong spirit of independence in their attitudes toward the Moroccan central government. Slightly more than three decades after the famed 1925 amphibious landing Franco took part in at Al Hoceima, discussed in the following chapter, the now-independent Moroccan government staged a similar landing in 1958 during its brutal military suppression of yet another Rif rebellion.

In 1909, however, the problems stemmed from Spanish mining and the construction of a railroad between Melilla and the mines to carry people, supplies, and the mined iron-ore and lead. The mining and construction provoked the violent resistance of some Moroccans, and in July they attacked Spanish workers at a railroad bridge, killing six and injuring one. In response, several thousand troops from the Melilla garrison marched out and drove away the attackers. The commander of the Spanish forces in Morocco, Gen. José Marina, also ordered a naval bombardment of coastal villages. From this point on Spanish troops protecting the mines faced repeated guerrilla harassment.

At the end of the month the situation turned disastrous for the Spaniards, when ill-prepared soldiers were sent to a very vulnerable area—known as Wolf Ravine (Barranco del Lobo)—to act against Rifian tribesmen who had sabotaged a railway line. The end result was more than a thousand Spanish casualties, including about 180 deaths.[3] As Franco must have realized when he heard of the disaster during the summer break before his last year as a cadet, Spanish military doctrine did not adequately address the conditions in Morocco.

Even those Spaniards who did not see large-scale action, such as that at Wolf Ravine, faced unfamiliar and unexpected dangers, in many ways similar to what American soldiers later faced in Vietnam and Afghanistan. As an unusually astute and articulate young Spanish artillery officer, Carlos Martínez de Campos, later wrote, most soldiers confronted a situation very different from what they had been told to expect. And one that didn't resemble any past wars with which they were familiar.

On the one hand it was what the officer, Carlos Martínez de Campos, called "pre-modern warfare," although at this point he believed its age was still not a great handicap thanks to the even poorer quality of the enemies' weapons and supplies. Especially striking was the contrast between the red and blue uniforms of the Spanish Hussars who escorted General Marina and the white robes of the Moroccan notables. The "shining sabers and the magnificent Moorish daggers," Martínez de Campos observed,

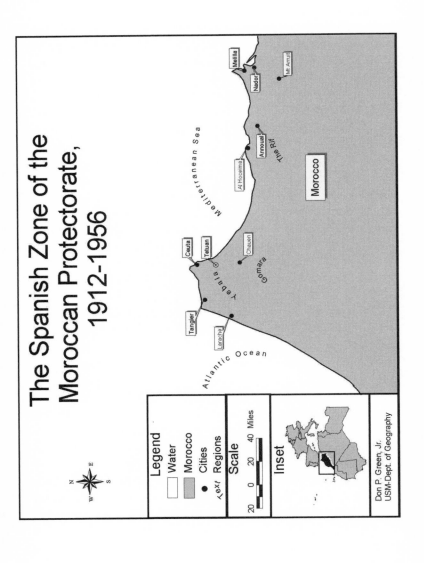

The Spanish Zone of the Moroccan Protectorate, 1912-1956

Mediterranean Sea

Atlantic Ocean

Tangier
Larache
Ceuta
Tetuan
Chauen
Yebala
Gomara
Al Hoceima
Annoual
The Rif
Nador
Melilla
Mt Arrud

Morocco

Legend
Water
Morocco
Cities
Text Regions

Scale
20   0   20   40 Miles

Inset

Don P. Green, Jr.
USM-Dept. of Geography

"harked back to another, more remote age." Generals still reviewed positions on horseback; to do so by car would have been considered unseemly.

But it was also "war without battles," in which soldiers had to endure excruciating boredom, standing guard and awaiting possible attacks that would only occur when and if their Moroccan opponents so desired. The Spaniards felt like "prisoners of inertia," digging trenches or setting up camp, and then simply waiting. On more than a few nights, riflemen heard sounds and fired at "invisible enemies," never to find out if any real enemy had actually been out there.

The Moroccans of the Rif employed classical guerrilla tactics, not unlike those of Mao in China, Ho Chi Minh in Vietnam, and the fighters in Afghanistan who have made life so difficult for Soviet and U.S. forces. The Moroccans knew how to make up for their lack of modern weaponry and supplies by avoiding contact with the Spaniards until the conditions were ideal for lightning but deadly attacks, which they followed with a quick retreat before their opponents could recover. The Rifians also understood how to use terror; they realized that killing Spaniards in isolated outposts and then leaving their bodies—sometimes mutilated—for other Spanish soldiers to find instilled great fear. In fact, a Berber proverb maintained that "victory comes not from the quantity of enemy deaths, but rather the number of frightened enemy forces." At night, moreover, the Moroccans controlled the countryside, and they were perfectly capable of waiting patiently in the mountains for the right time to descend and attack. Once armed with captured artillery and machine guns, the instinctive tactics of the Moroccans became even more worrisome.[4]

Franco himself felt the need to stress the differences between conventional warfare and the tactics of Moroccan guerrilla fighters even more than a decade after his first posting in North Africa. The Moroccans understood very well, he wrote, that many Spaniards lacked the necessary "craftiness of war," and that they rigidly followed regulations "without molding them to the

special nature of the combat." Officers thus needed to instruct
their men accordingly, Franco stressed, and the military units
themselves needed weapons more appropriate for Morocco.
Franco would advocate, for example, the heavy use of mortars
against an enemy that did its best to avoid open contact, preferring to hide out in gorges, ravines, and hollows.[5]

As Franco learned when he first came to North Africa in 1912,
even in areas supposedly under Spanish control it was not always
so easy to tell if the inhabitants had truly submitted. A decade
later this lesson became horribly apparent during the military
disaster near the town of Annoual, where Moroccan forces ostensibly on the side of the Spaniards joined in the slaughter of
thousands upon thousands of retreating Spanish soldiers. In the
Spanish Civil War Franco remembered the lessons of Morocco,
making sure his enemy was incapable of rearguard attacks by
brutally suppressing all possible forces of resistance before moving on to conquer more territory.

While he was still a cadet, the political turmoil caused by the
1909 Moroccan campaign made nearly as deep an impression on
Franco as the stories of the combat itself that spread around the
academy. The events in Spain during the summer of 1909, just
before his last year at the academy, certainly left their mark on
his still developing political consciousness. They not only served
as another example of the supposed dangers of Freemasonry, but
memories of the disorder and street violence to come out of that
summer's anti-war protests also reinforced his perception of socialist and anarchist treachery.

When Moroccan attacks on Spaniards escalated in July 1909,
Prime Minister Antonio Maura decided to bring in reserves, and
his Minister of War called up the Third Mixed Brigade of Chas-
seurs, composed of both active and reserve units. Among those
called up were 520 men who had completed their active duty six
years before and did not expect to serve again. The members of
the brigade came from Catalonia in northeastern Spain, whose
capital, Barcelona, was home to a large anarchist movement, the
antimonarchist Radical Republican Party, and many regional

nationalists who considered themselves more Catalan than Spanish.

The resulting antiwar protest in Barcelona turned into a week of violent rioting, street fighting, and strikes that must have horrified Franco. The rioters torched churches and convents, which they associated with the political status quo and wealthy classes they viewed as oppressors. Needless to say, the news of the looting and burning of convents shocked and deeply disturbed conservatives all over Spain. At the end of the month, the "Tragic Week," as it came to be known, came to an end, but only after the army was called up and many lives were lost. According to official statistics, when order was finally restored the army and police force had a final casualty count of eight dead and 124 wounded, while slightly over one hundred civilians lost their lives in the violence. Many army officers concluded from the experience that the Spanish political system of parliamentary government was ineffective, and that the increasingly violent workers' movements posed dangers that only they could put down.[6]

Franco seems to have drawn another lesson from the Morocco-related turmoil as well. By the time the first Melilla campaign finally ended in late November of 1909, the government of Prime Minister Maura had fallen. Considered by many conservatives as one of the most promising of Spain's politicians, Maura had at first refused to resign after the Tragic Week, despite calls from the opposition to do so. For Spaniards on the political right, Maura seemed the only Spanish leader who might be strong enough to restore Spain's political and social health. But his enemies held him responsible for the Tragic Week and its consequences, including the subsequent military trial and execution of the alleged instigator of the Tragic Week, Francisco Ferrer.

Many conservative Spaniards viewed Ferrer as a subversive, freethinking advocate of dangerous political doctrine and free love, and they believed the secular, libertine school he had founded in Barcelona to be morally dangerous. But his advocates all over the rest of Europe saw him as a victim of a new incarnation of the Spanish Inquisition, and protests on his behalf took place in many countries. Monuments to him were even erected in some cities; one still stands in Brussels. Meanwhile, back in Spain members of the Liberal and Leftist Republican Parties called for Maura's resignation in the wake of the Tragic Week.[7]

Yet the Tragic Week was not a reflection of how all Spaniards reacted to the 1909 fighting in Morocco. For Franco and many others, the events in Morocco—including the well-publicized loss of Wolf Ravine—triggered patriotism and a desire to fight. It also had support from the middle and upper classes, which later provided Franco with much of his political base. Newspapers ran stories of young aristocrats who volunteered to join the soldiers in Morocco, an especially newsworthy act in a country with a long tradition of avoidance of the draft by all but the poor. The law that allowed draftees to pay a fee to avoid military service was suspended. When the Spaniards finally returned to Wolf Ravine, the planting of the flag on Mount Gurugú above it stirred much fanfare. The story of a corporal who, captured by the Moroccans, sacrificed his own life to save those of his comrades, also became the stuff of legend.

In the end, though, the king yielded to pressures and withdrew his support for Prime Minister Maura in October. According to many Spanish conservatives then and now, Freemasons fueled the anti-Maura forces. In Franco's mind, Freemasonry was thus related to yet another unfortunate event in Spanish history—this time the fall of an able conservative politician. When he himself led Spain years later, the apparent threat posed by Freemasonry continued to haunt him.[8]

In the meantime, though, Franco had to make a name for himself through his actions in the place where Maura's serious troubles had begun: North Africa. His first days there, however, were not particularly auspicious. After arriving in Melilla in mid-February 1912, he passed his time quietly before reporting to his new assignment in the Sixty-eighth Africa Regiment, under the command of the former director of the Infantry Academy during his days as a cadet, Col. José Villalba Riquelme. Unlike many of his colleagues, Franco chose not to take part in the opportunities for drinking and whoring that surrounded him. The reputation that he soon gained as a colonial officer lacked these kinds of excesses, although many Spanish soldiers in Morocco partook of the temptations, which were often close at hand.

In fact, many officers were corrupt and uncaring about the well-being of the troops, who were themselves overwhelmingly poor, unmotivated, illiterate, and poorly trained. Franco even claimed that he spent his first night with his men without sleeping, with a pistol in his hand for fear of what they might do.[9] Many of Franco's fellow officers, moreover, were hardly setting a good example for their soldiers. As an especially critical captain later wrote, these officers

> spent their time whoring and gambling in Melilla. . . . Some officers never saw their regiments, but contented themselves with parading like peacocks through the streets while the half-starved youths of Spain in shoddy, torn clothes wandered miserably through the Riff hills, not knowing where they were going or even why they were engaged in this fantastic adventure.[10]

Franco himself, along with a good many of his colleagues from the officer corps, may not have behaved so badly or sought to avoid combat. Nevertheless, many others did so, and widespread corruption, graft, fraud, and other ills persisted.[11]

Franco's identity was that of a more highly motivated and professionally-minded *africanista*, a term usually used to designate the ambitious officers serving in Morocco who fervently believed in Spain's imperial mission there. As Franco later told an interviewer, "Even I can't understand myself without Africa." And, in fact, he did his job there with very impressive enthusiasm and dedication. Not many military officers can say that they have taken part in fifty combat operations during the course of their career, but Franco could make that claim about his time in Africa.[12] Later, as dictator, he cultivated this image of his *africanista* background. He even appeared at public functions accompanied by his "Moorish

Guard," an honor guard composed of traditionally-dressed Moroccan soldiers who reinforced an image of colonialist exoticism.

Yet Franco was not an *africanista* in the same sense as some of his colleagues, who combined a deep interest in Morocco and its cultures with a belief in Spain's civilizing mission as an imperial power. He certainly believed in Spain's historic rights to a North African empire, and he would angrily reject any suggestion of relinquishing the Moroccan territory that had taken the lives of so many of his colleagues. But his professional goals were the main reason he served there so energetically—he did not view Moroccan service as an end in itself, but rather as a way to attain greater heights for himself in the Spanish army. In fact, after July 1936 he never returned to the land of his most formative years as a soldier. Although he would make a brief visit to Ifni and the Spanish Sahara to the south in 1950, after departing for mainland Spain at the start of the civil war, he never returned to the Moroccan protectorate.[13]

Franco's first North African posting, in February 1912, coincided with the official establishment of the Moroccan "protectorate," which was the legal term for what was in essence a colony under mostly indirect French and Spanish rule. The Spanish zone in the protectorate—formally established in November—was smaller and poorer than that of the French, stretching along the northern Mediterranean coast. It consisted of about 18,000 square miles, with many clans and subclans occupying its land. These groups were loosely organized into sixty-six larger tribes, but the clans and subclans often entered into conflicts with one another.[14] Thus, in spite of the Spanish zone's small size, developments there would be very complicated and often deadly.

Spain's military actions took place in what were essentially two separate theaters of operations. The first was centered on the western side of the protectorate around Tetuan, which the Spaniards designated as the capital of their zone. Spanish military activities there and in the surrounding, mountainous area of the Yebala aimed primarily at establishing and maintaining a semblance of order and control. This goal required a solid presence in the so-called unsubmitted areas, including Tetuan itself, which was actually still unoccupied when the protectorate was established.

In 1913 the Spaniards occupied Tetuan. In this case, at least, the Spanish operation definitely did *not* exemplify the unimaginative, primitive, and brutal types of tactics that critics argued were typical of Spain's occupation of Morocco. The taking of Tetuan was made possible by a combination of extreme caution, the winning over of some local leaders, very secret planning, and outward respect for Moroccan culture. The Spanish high commissioner, Gen. Felipe Alfau, had not even told all Spanish officers about the final objective of their operation, and he had striven to win over the local pasha with gifts and even military decorations. His orders had forbidden soldiers from stopping in front of mosques, staring at women, or offending the religious sensibilities of the city's inhabitants in general. As a result of these measures, his troops were able to enter the city in February without firing a shot. He erred, however, in escorting the new caliph into the city, which made the caliph seem like a puppet of the Spaniards. Needless to say, this continues to be a common mistake of western armies that occupy Muslim lands; in the case of Spanish Morocco, many local leaders had to tread a fine line if they hoped to keep any credibility whatsoever with their own people.[15]

In any case, the occupation of Tetuan did not give the Spaniards much time to relax. Even if many of Tetuan's residents preferred occupation by the Spaniards to the rule of some of their own country's brutal chieftains, nearby Moroccan leaders were not so happy about the foreign incursion. They thus fomented what to the Spaniards was a surprising amount of violent resistance, some of which Franco encountered firsthand. Matters were not helped, moreover, by the reappearance of the famed warlord El Raisuni as a significant resistor to Spanish actions.[16]

The sharif Muley Ahmed el Raisuni was the leader of the Beni Arós tribe, but in fact, his power in Morocco extended well beyond the confines of the tribe. At one point his actions had even provoked a strong reaction from U.S. President Theodore Roosevelt. Roosevelt sent two cruisers to the Moroccan coast after El Raisuni kidnapped the Greek millionaire Ion Perdicaris, who claimed to be an American, and the British diplomats Walter Harris and Sir Harry McLean. But the cruisers alone did not do the trick; El Raisuni received large ransoms and other concessions in the end for the release of his captives.

Yet El Raisuni was far more than just a high-level bandit; he was also one of the most powerful political figures in all of North Africa. Because he claimed to descend from the patron saint of Morocco, Muley Idris, he belonged to the network of the country's top religious leaders. This status in turn gave him special privileges. Although he had suffered at the hands of the sultan of Morocco and other rivals, by the time Franco arrived in the country, El Raisuni had reestablished himself and become a very powerful leader. In fact, the sultan found it expedient to confer upon him official status as a regional representative of the Moroccan state.

The Spaniards found El Raisuni to be a significant obstacle to their efforts to gain control of their zone in the protectorate. His treatment of enemy Moroccan prisoners was shockingly brutal even to hardened Spanish officers, and he enriched himself and maintained control over his territory by combining taxation, extortion, and violent repression with claims to be defending the values of Islam against Christian European invaders. Because he was such a powerful figure, the Spaniards had little choice but to deal with him, and Lt. Col. Manuel Fernández Silvestre made an agreement meant to guarantee peaceful relations between his forces and the Spaniards. Inevitably, though, the deal fell apart with time, and El Raisuni's forces caused major difficulties for years to come by resisting the Spanish occupiers. These difficulties put Franco in mortal danger on more than one occasion.

But at first the deal with El Raisuni seemed to yield positive results for the Spaniards, ending much of the on-going, small-scale fighting that had taken place between his forces and the Spaniards. In return for enjoying essentially a free reign in the mountains, El

Raisuni had held off his attacks on the Spanish troops. Silvestre went as far as to recommend that he be made caliph. The situation had clearly benefited the muley, who saw his authority grow while he continued to remain independent of Spanish control. Furthermore, Spanish occupation of a limited number of towns, forts, and other scattered posts had hardly been tantamount to establishing authority on land ideal for guerrilla operations. As El Raisuni later remarked, "With you, if a town is taken, that is the end. With us it means a few more men in the mountains."

In the meantime, Franco entered combat for the first time in the eastern Spanish zone of the Moroccan protectorate. The eastern theater was based around Melilla, although it would eventually extend farther south and westwards into the Rif and toward Al Hoceima Bay. Here Franco was removed from the drama of Tetuan and Chauen. Years later, when the major hostilities took place in the east, Franco was in the west, again removed, at least at first, from the major drama in Spanish North Africa—this time around Annoual. Nevertheless, Franco experienced plenty of danger and excitement in both theaters. In fact, he did not have to wait long to go into combat after first arriving in Melilla in February 1912.

His baptism of fire, or first combat experience, took place as part of the Kert River campaign in the eastern Rif. The Kert River extends from the Mediterranean coast west of Melilla to the south. The Spaniards had been threatened by Rifian tribesmen commanded by a local sheikh, known as El Mezian, who had declared a *jihad* against the occupying Christians. The Spanish goal was to extend their control west of the river, thereby helping to secure the safety of the mining areas and the communications routes to Melilla. At the same time, the campaign aimed to remove Melilla itself from possible threats. The Fort of Tifasor, where Franco joined field operations, constituted part of the outer defense of Melilla.

He received his orders on 24 February to join Colonel Villalba's regiment. Upon Franco's arrival, the colonel's first order was to cover his shiny sword scabbard, which could serve as a target to snipers. But even en route to the fort Franco, along with the other inexperienced young officers who accompanied him, saw firsthand the possible consequences of the impending dangers: veterans who had already been wounded and were now returning to combat joined the young, novice officers in the short journey from Melilla.

The dangers became even more apparent to Franco the next month, when he found himself in command of a platoon (*sección*) that formed part of a small column, taking the advance guard in a reconnaissance operation over the Kert River. In this operation he had his first direct combat experience. The Spanish losses in the campaign were so high that the Madrid government, hoping to ward off criticism of the war at home, chose to end it and call for a withdrawal in May. Some officers later remembered the withdrawal with much bitterness, arguing that they had been making good progress. They had already pushed the Rifians back across the Kert River and killed El Mezian. The officers found the situation even more infuriating when the enemy troops began to sing of victory as the Spaniards withdrew. The whole affair provided for young, highly motivated officers like Franco what seemed like yet another example of the damage wrought by civilian interference in military affairs.[17]

In June 1912 Franco was promoted to first lieutenant, the only promotion he ever received based entirely on seniority. His combat merits made possible all others. His opportunities for combat increased after he applied for a transfer to the newly established native security forces, the *Regulares Indígenas*. The *Regulares* were Moroccans who fought under the command of Spanish officers in return for regular pay, and they and their officers soon earned a reputation as excellent and fierce fighters. Often at the vanguard of attacks, they provided the perfect setting for Franco to develop his reputation for calm and courage under fire. In April 1913 he finally received his posting to the *Regulares,* shortly after the Spanish occupation of Larache.

Franco's incorporation into the *Regulares* soon brought him to the western part of the protectorate's Spanish zone, near Ceuta and Tetuan. The strategic situation in which he now found himself was far from ideal. The deal that had kept El Raisuni relatively docile was disintegrating, and rebellions had spread through a number of *cabilas* in the central and western parts of the Spanish zone. Rebel Moroccans now posed a threat to Tetuan, Larache, and Alcazarquivir, although in the end the Spaniards retained control of all three.

But protecting the lines of communication between these towns was a difficult and deadly affair. Under constant danger of enemy sniper fire, the Spaniards built small wooden blockhouses, each protected by sandbags and barbed wire. A platoon of about twenty men garrisoned each blockhouse, and they lived in frightening isolation, receiving provisions of food, water, and firewood every few days. The blockhouses, which were rarely larger than twelve by eighteen feet, lacked storage and sanitation facilities. Bringing supplies to the blockhouses was, of course, a dangerous task in itself, thanks to the possibility of ambushes and snipers.

Franco later stressed the need for careful, cautious planning, supply, and execution for the rapid construction of lines of fortifications and other positions in Morocco. Such prudence was necessary, he argued, to ensure that the Spanish positions interacted together in mutual support. Although he later led his men on a white horse from time to time, in Morocco he gained a reputation as a careful officer in general who stressed planning, security, logistics, and knowledge of terrain.

He also exhibited strong leadership skills in spite of his young age. Years later, in a broader operational context, Franco displayed the same inclination toward careful planning, prudence, and system-level thought that he had revealed as a young officer in Morocco. During the civil war, he clearly favored moving on to take more territory only after achieving complete control and mutual security against enemy attacks in the towns and cities he conquered.

Almost immediately after his posting with the *Regulares,* Franco went into combat, taking part in four operations in July. In late September he participated in the hard combat around the

so-called Izarduy position, named after the captain who had fortified and then died defending it. The after-action report by the
general in chief specifically praised the role played by Franco's
company in what it portrayed as the heroic recovery of Izarduy's
body. As a result of this and his other noteworthy actions, in October Franco was decorated with a Red Cross of Military Merit,
First Class—the first of many honors he received during his military career.

On the first day of February 1914, he exhibited noteworthy
bravery in a battle near Tetuan, aimed at repulsing a dangerously
deep penetration by Moroccan enemies toward that city. This
operation proved a hard test for the *Regulares*, but one from
which they emerged victorious and thereby solidified their reputation for highly effective fighting. As a result of his actions during this difficult day, Franco received a promotion to captain one
year later that was retroactively effective from the date of the battle.[18]

In June 1916 Franco took part in a battle near Ceuta during
which he came very close to dying. Guerrillas had threatened the
Spanish town by taking positions in the hills around it, which
induced the Spaniards to conduct a large-scale sweep of the area
to remove the threat. As their Moroccan enemies expected, the
Spaniards decided to attack El Biutz, a village perched at the top
of a mountain. Franco joined the company that spearheaded the
advance up the hill, taking heavy fire from the enemy trenches
above. As the company advanced, tribesmen made their way
down the other side of the mountain and then moved around
the attacking Spaniards in a surprise encirclement.

During the fight Franco took over the leadership of the company after its commander was badly wounded, and he managed
to break out of the encirclement. He helped the Spaniards to triumph and take El Biutz, but not without many Spanish casualties. One of the fallen Spaniards was Franco himself, who took a
very serious gunshot wound to the stomach.

The wound was so serious that he was not expected to survive
it. He probably only did so because the medical officer at the

nearby first aid station refused to allow his transfer to Ceuta's military hospital, believing that his condition was still too precarious to endure the short journey. Thanks to the medical officer's orders, Franco remained for two weeks at the aid station, during which time he recovered enough to survive the move to the hospital when it finally came. He had been extremely lucky; the gunshot had missed vital organs by less than an inch. The accident seemed to prove that Franco was blessed with what his Moroccan troops called *baraka*, a sort of magical or spiritual quality that he encouraged his men to believe he had.

In the wake of his wounding, Franco's actions made it clear that ample self-pride and personal ambition went along with his dedication and bravery. The high commissioner of Morocco, Gen. Francisco Gómez-Jordana, recommended Franco's promotion to major, and his office also began the process of awarding Franco with Spain's most distinguished decoration for bravery, the Gran Cruz Laureada de San Fernando. But the Ministry of War opposed both moves, believing that they were inappropriate for an officer only twenty-three years old. The ministry may have also viewed the extremely high praise of Franco in the after-action report as a bit of an exaggeration, since it seemed to have been written with the assumption that Franco would not survive his injury.

In any case, Franco's response was highly audacious, demonstrating his own high sense of self worth and his unwillingness to accept political decisions that stood in his way: he appealed to the king, asking the high commissioner to support his request. Although he did not receive the decoration, his bold move paid off professionally, and in late February his promotion to major was made official. The promotion was retroactive, moreover, valid from late June 1916.

Although Franco was pleased with his promotion, it meant that he had to leave Morocco, where there were no vacant positions for majors. Franco's success at such a young age would again cause him difficulties shortly thereafter, when he applied to the staff college (the *Escuela Superior de Guerra,* or Superior

War College). This time he was turned down because his rank was already too high to register for the classes, which were aimed at the best young officers of his age.[19]

His posting was now in Oviedo in the region of Asturias, to the east of his native Galicia. At this post he would meet his future wife, María del Carmen Polo y Martínez Valdés. When the military governor of the area, Gen. Ricardo Burguete, declared martial law in response to a strike in the late summer of 1917, Franco headed one of the military columns he sent into action. The military suppression of the Asturian strike was brutal, resulting in around eighty deaths, 150 wounded, and 2,000 arrests. Many of the arrested workers, moreover, were brutally tortured. But despite subsequent assertions by his enemies, Franco's column may not have taken part in any of the violence, as Franco himself later claimed.[20] In the same region of Asturias years later, though, during the strikes and revolutionary upheaval of 1934, Franco played a leading role in another infamous military suppression.

At this point, however, Franco was best known for his feats in North Africa. He was clearly proud of his record there, as his attempt in the early 1920s to take advantage of his reputation as an *africanista* made clear. Although he was not the only officer in the Spanish army to have survived a near-fatal wound and to have exhibited leadership skills, bravery, and calm in combat, his record was undeniably one of the most impressive in the officer corps. He could justifiably feel proud of how far he had come since graduating from the Infantry Academy in such a poor position a few years before. He also saw Spain's actions in North Africa in a considerably more positive light than many critics then and now, and it is important to remember that he was not alone in his assessment.

In retrospect, it is not hard to criticize the Spanish commanders in Morocco, and frequently with good reason. Spain's military actions in North Africa had, moreover, very unpleasant consequences for the indigenous peoples on more than a few occasions, as was the case in many European colonial adventures.

But the horrible disaster the Spaniards would experience at An-nual in 1921 should not overshadow completely the military successes that they had achieved in North Africa. Nor should it obscure the context of the deadly errors at tactical, operational, and strategic levels that other military commanders all over Europe committed during this period.

As can be said about the after-the-fact critiques of military blundering in World War I, it is possible to go too far when stressing the endemic problems and errors of the Spanish military. In the case of World War I, many historians now question previous condemnations of the so-called donkey generals for causing the bloodbaths of the western front. Even the traditional perception of the 1916 Battle of the Somme as a prime example of bad military leadership, futility, and the horrors of modern war has come under critical scrutiny.[21]

The history of the Moroccan protectorate is certainly not devoid of widespread corruption, horrible treatment of troops, bad decisions, and other misguided, negligent, and incompetent actions that cost many lives—often needlessly so. Suffering from considerable material failings, the Spanish army in Morocco was indeed inferior to its French, German, and British colonial counterparts, among others. But acknowledging the failures of Spanish military endeavors does not have to entail completely overlooking their successes or the international context in which they operated.

Not surprisingly, Franco himself later portrayed the learning curve of Spanish officers in Morocco in a more positive light than the critics. He argued that the Moroccan war helped rid the Spanish military of "archaic rules and regulations and the old prejudices and routines of years of garrison life, making possible and constituting a new school of combat, perfected by necessity." For this reason, he claimed, by 1913 and early 1914 the Spaniards had already developed precursors to the artillery tactics later brought to fruition during World War I.[22]

Of course, this attempt by Franco to put a positive spin on the initial faults of Spanish military operations in Morocco was rather self-serving, and he exaggerated when describing the skills of the Spanish artillery corps. He also glossed over earlier Spanish military blunders. And, most tellingly, he implied that officers without strong theoretical or academic military skills but with ample down-to-earth experience—in other words, officers like himself—were most valuable. Nevertheless, when Franco first returned to Africa in 1920, this time with the newly-formed Spanish Foreign Legion, he could justifiably assert that Spanish military effectiveness in Morocco had greatly improved since he had first set foot there nearly eight years before. As he would soon discover, though, there was still a lot to be learned.

The Rising Star

When Franco returned to North Africa in October 1920, he did so as the second in command of the recently created Spanish Foreign Legion. Recruitment had only begun early the previous month for this new fighting force, officially designated the *Tercio de Extranjeros* but referred to by Franco and most others as simply *La Legión*. It quickly gained fame as a tough and effective force, with a battlefield reputation that exceeded even that of the *Regulares*. The Legion also became known for the sheer brutality of its soldiers, off the battlefield as well as on it. On their first night in Ceuta, soldiers from the first *bandera* (battalion), which was under Franco's command, made their presence known in an especially violent fashion: the night's upheaval included the murders of a prostitute and a corporal of the guard.[1]

The founder and commander in chief of the Legion was José Millán-Astray, one of twentieth-century Europe's most colorful military figures. He later found a place in Spanish history as the one-eyed, one-armed general who assaulted the famous writer Miguel de Unamuno with cries of "Death to the Intelligentsia!"

at a banquet. In the ensuing turmoil, Franco's wife had to escort the elderly writer from the building. But even well before this incident, which took place during the first year of the Spanish Civil War, Millán-Astray and the Legion had already attracted considerable attention in Spain and North Africa. Their fame—or infamy—persists to this day.

As late as the 1990s, a bottle with what is said to be the remains of Millán-Astray's extracted eye was on display in the Legion's museum in Ceuta. This grotesque relic of the Legion's founder, who continued to extol war and death even after losing an arm and an eye in combat, graphically symbolizes what the Legion stood for. The organization that Franco entered in 1920 was even more extreme than that of the *Regulares*, and no one better personified it than Millán-Astray himself.

From the beginning, the founder of the Legion exalted danger and death in highly spiritual terms. The Legion's motto, "Legionnaires, to fight; Legionnaires, to die," was no empty phrase. Indeed, the Legionnaire's Creed, as Millán-Astray later wrote, proclaimed death in combat to be "the highest honor." Custom called for the soldiers to respond to the requests from their officers for "Volunteers to die" by shouting "Everyone!" in unison. The soldiers themselves took the epithet "bridegrooms of death."

This kind of morbid, violent rhetoric soon manifested itself in a very real way through the growing acceptance by Franco and others of brutality and inhumanity on the battlefield. One legionnaire, for example, later described how his colleagues ripped the entrails out of their fallen enemies and cut off their victims' ears and heads, which they then stabbed with their bayonets and carried with them. When a duchess organized a team of nurses as an act of charity, a group of legionnaires felt it appropriate to express their gratitude with a basket of roses—in the middle of which lay two severed Moroccan heads. According to some accounts, in 1926, dictator Primo de Rivera was shocked to discover that some of the legionnaires he was inspecting had human heads stuck on their bayonets.[2]

Volunteers from the United States, Britain, Germany, and other countries who enlisted in the Legion found life under the command of Millán-Astray and his officers even harder than they had expected. They complained that they were not paid as promised and that they suffered "cruel disciplinary measures." According to a report from the U.S. consulate general in Madrid, these measures included being "burdened with rocks" and forced to go into action tied to one another.

As a result of such hardships, eighty Americans—many of whom were U.S. Army or Navy veterans—joined British subjects in seeking official help to return home.[3] Perhaps because of the conditions, only about 30 percent of the legionnaires were foreigners, including a "gigantic black man from New York" and "an 'undesirable' Belgian" among the initial recruits. Among the motivations that had inspired the recruits to sign up, Millán-Astray wrote, was "a desire to die."

The environment of the Legion only served to reinforce Franco's emotional coldness and indifference to suffering. It also further strengthened his tendency toward an aloof and coldly rational "military" approach to problems. As an officer in the *Regulares*, he had ordered his Moroccan soldiers beaten for minor infractions. In the Legion he went as far as to calmly order the shooting of deserters and insubordinate soldiers. This willingness to mete out drastic punishments foreshadowed the brutal lack of mercy he would show toward prisoners, including his own cousin, during the civil war. As he told another cousin years later, on one occasion he successfully restored discipline in his Legion battalion by making his soldiers march past the body of a fellow legionnaire whom he had ordered shot on the spot for insubordination.

Although Franco had no tolerance for improper behavior directed at him or his officers, he was much more lenient when his soldiers committed acts of violence against others. Along with their paternalistic indulgence, he and the Legion's other officers believed in the positive effects of the terror that such actions could produce. Their lenience toward the crimes of their men had its antecedent in the behavior that officers had allowed in the *Regulares*. In part to keep their Moroccan soldiers happy and prevent them from deserting, the officers had sometimes allowed them to rob, rape, and commit other crimes as they passed through villages, which they sometimes set aflame after pillaging. In addition to satisfying the soldiers' desire for booty, these actions were meant to frighten other would-be resistors to Spanish rule.[4]

Franco was certainly not the only colonial officer to rely on terror to help make occupied peoples submit; it is an integral element of much colonial military history. In a sense, moreover, when his soldiers mutilated enemy corpses, killed, and pillaged, they were simply committing a closer and more personal variation of the merciless torching and bombing from the air of indigenous villages—a practice the Spaniards shared with the French and Italians in North Africa. Franco later transferred this concept back to his own country during the Spanish Civil War, directing the terror against fellow Spaniards. In the civil war his German allies also employed fear-inspiring tactics against civilians, including the bombing of urban areas from the air. And shortly thereafter, the military's use of terror against civilians reached new heights during World War II.

Franco probably gave scant thought, however, to the broader context of Spanish tactical developments in Morocco when he set foot there again in 1920. His more immediate goal was to succeed in his position as the second in command of the Legion. His actions formed part of a broader strategic picture that had evolved somewhat since his last African posting. From 1919 onward the Spaniards adopted a more aggressive military policy in the entire protectorate. This new approach would bring with it truly disastrous consequences in the eastern theater, but at the time the situation did not look so bad.

In the spring of 1920, as Rifian resistance steadily grew, the new commandant general of the Melilla zone, Gen. Manuel Fernández Silvestre, had begun to advance and gain control of more territory. In theory, Silvestre's actions should have fit within the strategy of the protectorate's high commissioner since early 1919, Gen. Dámaso Berenguer. The high commissioner's strategy aimed to take control first of the territory in the Yebala region of the western sector between the coastal cities of Ceuta, on the Mediterranean across from Gibraltar, and Larache, on the Atlantic. After the Spaniards had established domination in the interior of the Yebala, Spanish forces in the east were to move out from Melilla to occupy and control their sector. The logical culmination of these moves would be the eventual creation of a territorial link between the eastern and western theaters and Spanish control of the whole protectorate.

As Berenguer moved early to secure the territory between Tetuan and the Atlantic coast, a recent reorganization of the protectorate's command structure allowed Silvestre in the east to operate more or less independently of the big picture and ahead of the game. Silvestre could thus advance westward with such haste that he stretched thin his supply lines and exposed his flanks. His method contrasted greatly with the cautious approach of Berenguer, who personally directed operations in the Yebala. Berenguer preferred to move slowly and negotiate simultaneously with local tribes. His methods, although slow, yielded the desired results. Between September and October he took El Fondak, a key position on the road between Tetuan and Tangiers, and by the end of October he had occupied the city of Chauen (*Xauen*). By the beginning of July 1921, he appeared on the verge of capturing Raisuni.[5]

The occupation of Chauen had been especially impressive. Nestled in the mountains about sixty miles south of Tetuan, Chauen is considered a holy place for all Muslims. At the time when the Spanish zone of the protectorate was drawn up, only three Europeans were said to have set foot in the town, which had reputedly been founded by Andalusians expelled from Spain in the fifteenth century. These Europeans had been forced to enter the town in disguise in order to avoid being killed.

Chauen's occupation by Spanish forces in 1920 resulted in

large part from the endeavors of Col. Alberto Castro Girona, who had some knowledge and understanding of the area and its cultures. Castro Girona was also known as an advocate of more peaceful approaches to the conquest of Moroccan territory. In this case his method consisted of entering the town alone in the disguise of a charcoal-burner and then walking into a meeting of local notables. He told the notables that Spanish columns had surrounded the town, even though fewer columns had actually reached the town's outskirts than he claimed. He also used bribes to win favor with the inhabitants. The local leaders thus let the Spaniards occupy the city.

When the Spanish forces entered the city, they received a warm welcome from the local Jewish community. The Jews of Chauen traced their origins to ancestors expelled by Ferdinand and Isabel in 1492, the same year that Christopher Columbus made his famous voyage to the American continent. Speaking an old Spanish dialect that was probably Ladino, they presented the Spaniards with large iron keys that they believed had been passed down to them by their ancestors. These keys, they said, had belonged to synagogues and houses in Granada before the expulsion of the Jews.[6]

The manner in which Castro Girona orchestrated the peaceful rendition of Chauen clearly made an impression on Franco. Although the future dictator may have differed from Castro Girona in many ways, he respected him and wrote very positively of his good relations with Moroccans. Castro Girona, in turn, sided with Franco when the Spanish Civil War broke out in 1936.[7]

The successes in the Yebala came to an end just as the Spaniards surrounded El Raisuni at Tazarut, when attention unexpectedly shifted to the eastern theater. Early in the morning of 22 July 1921, Franco received orders to move his *bandera* toward Fondak de Ain Yedida and then Tetuan. Responding immediately to the urgency of the orders, Franco commanded his troops on a grueling forced march so intense that it resulted in the deaths of two of his men. When he arrived in Tetuan, news was already spreading of a terrible military defeat in the eastern theater of the Spanish zone. The situation was so bad that General Silvestre had died—possibly by suicide—at the head of his troops. Franco and his men immediately joined the second *bandera* on a train for Ceuta, where they then boarded a steamer for Melilla.[8]

El Raisuni had been saved by one of the worst military disasters in the history of modern European colonialism—the costliest in lives experienced by a European colonial army since the Italian defeat at Adowa in 1896. Back in the eastern part of the protectorate, the forward positions of Silvestre's troops, based around the village of Annoual, suffered fierce attacks by forces organized by the Rifian rebel leader Abd al-Karim al-Khattabi. The subsequent withdrawal of the Spanish troops turned into a panic and a rout when tribes in the area joined in the slaughter as the Spaniards tried to flee eastward toward Melilla. By 9 August at least 8,000 Spanish troops were dead, including Silvestre himself, in what became known as the disaster of Annoual. The Spanish soldiers and camp followers who were killed at the hands of the Moroccans often suffered horrible deaths, only to endure further mutilations postmortem.[9]

Upon their arrival, Franco and his men could do little except protect Melilla itself. As Franco wrote in his diary, the people of Melilla greeted the legionnaires very warmly, regardless of their reputation for violent carousing. The inhabitants of Melilla knew that the situation was extremely grave, and their fears and desires for revenge superceded all other sentiments. Although Mount Arruit, Nador, and Zeluán, all close to Melilla, fell to Abd al-Karim's troops, with the help of the Legion Melilla itself remained in Spanish hands. With Melilla secured, Franco then joined other legionnaires in the slow and gradual retaking of lost ground.

In fact, Franco now directed operations on the ground as commander of the first and second *banderas*, since Millán-Astray was temporarily in Madrid promoting the Legion and enlisting soldiers for two more recently created *banderas*. On 15 August Franco led an attack on the village of Sidi Amaran, forgoing promised artillery support. The Legion took the village at the cost of three Spanish lives.

Franco then revealed his belief in sowing terror to discourage further enemy aggression and to punish disloyalty. He requested and received permission from the high commissioner, Gen. José Sanjurjo, to conduct punitive attacks on the Moroccans who had acted against the Spaniards. Setting fire to their homes and putting the villagers themselves to the knife, his men employed many of the methods that Spaniards in Loyalist zones feared from Franco's Army of Africa during the civil war a decade and a half later.

In other ways as well, the Spanish reconquest of lost territory foreshadowed, albeit on a smaller scale, some of the same military techniques that the world would soon see in the Spanish Civil War and then World War II. Involving a coordinated combination of two columns of ground forces, an air squadron, heavy artillery from two battleships, floating batteries, land-based artillery, and an observation balloon, the Spanish offensive on the town of Nador provided Franco with important experience in operational-level command. In fact, his position in the chain of command rose to the top when Millán-Astray, who had returned from his trip to Madrid, received a bullet in the chest while conferring with Franco. Once again, Millán-Astray would survive his battle wound, but in the meantime Franco took command of the Legion.[10]

Besieged Spaniards were still holding out in Nador when the Legion arrived in Melilla, but because of more immediate needs in Melilla itself, they were left to their fate at the hands of the attacking Rifians, who finally took the town. As Franco and his men discovered, that fate was horrifying. Spaniards found similar scenes in the other areas they reoccupied. Army engineer Arturo Barea subsequently described what it was like to dispose of the thousands of bodies:

> Those dead we were finding when they had lain for days under the African sun which turned fresh meat putrid within two hours; those mummified dead whose bodies had burst; those mutilated bodies,

without eyes and tongues, their genitals defiled, violated with the
stakes from the barbed wire, their hands tied up with their own
bowels, beheaded, armless, legless, sawed in two—oh those dead!

Franco later commented that during this fighting near Melilla,
"the women were the most cruel, finishing off the wounded and
stripping them of their clothes, in this way paying back the wel-
fare that civilization brought them."[11] He apparently did not
consider that the "civilization" that the Spaniards had brought
Morocco had not always been wanted or benign.

Although Franco allowed his own men to commit atrocities
against their enemies, he was not so tolerant of battlefield excesses when Spaniards themselves were the victims, especially on
such an enormous scale. Instead, he wanted revenge. After a
massacre of Spaniards by insurgent Rifians at Dar Drius, he requested to enter the village and mete out punishment, but this
time his petition for vengeance was turned down. He got his
chance, however, when a blockhouse near Dar Drius came under
attack. Although his entire detachment had volunteered to come
to the rescue, Franco chose only twelve men to join him in re-
pelling the attack by tribesmen. The next day he and his men returned triumphant, carrying twelve bloody Moroccan heads as
proof of their exploits.[12]

Yet Franco's active life on the battlefield did not bring with it
a total divorce from the world of politics. The Legion as a whole
benefited from its well-publicized successes and sacrifices in the
wake of Annoual, and Franco was increasingly aware of his own
public image in Spain as a war hero. He also knew his stake in
the politics of the Spanish armed forces.

Within the army itself, the issue of merit promotions and
their threat to the traditional system of seniority lay behind
much of the political infighting. The conflict was complex, and
officers often had more than one reason for the positions they
took. But in general most of the so-called *africanista* officers like
Franco favored the merit promotions from which they had personally benefited so greatly. On the other side, many junior officers and others with little or no combat time in Morocco tended

to favor the traditional system of promotion through seniority. These officers in favor of promotion by seniority formed the so-called *Juntas de Defensa*, which was more or less akin to a labor union.

The *Juntas* had already influenced policymakers in Madrid far more than many other officers liked. Moreover, their initial opposition to the founding of the Legion itself, based on their fear of the creation of new elite units, had done little to improve their image among Franco and Millán-Astray. In March 1922 the *Juntas* went as far as to insist upon compulsory unionization and the renunciation of all merit promotions awarded after 30 April 1921—a date that fell several months before the disaster of Annoual.

When the government caved in to these demands, Franco joined a large group of officers who resigned in protest. Revealing a growing awareness of the importance of public opinion, he and Millán-Astray announced their decisions to resign in indignant letters, which were widely reprinted in the Spanish press. The public pressure they thereby generated had a strong effect on subsequent government policies.

Franco had actively sought to influence national politics, and he had succeeded, thanks in no small part to the positive media attention he was already enjoying. His role in the reoccupation of Nador had already earned him and colleagues like Millán-Astray much positive media attention, which in turn helped sway public opinion even more against the *Juntas*. In January the influential Spanish newspaper *ABC* had published a photo of him with the caption "Franco: the Legion's Ace."[13] Quite clearly, Franco's prominence in the public sphere was rising.

Yet his public image exceeded that of a soldier, and this was the identity he sought to project throughout his life. In his own mind, Franco probably perceived his actions as completely apolitical, but this interpretation reflected his traditionally military conception of politics. Like more than a few of his colleagues, he believed the Spanish army—or at least the sector of the army that shared his outlook—to be the true representative of the Spanish

nation. In his mind, *politics* was a word that referred to the ostensibly more self-centered actions of civilians in government. According to this view, what was best for him and the army was best
for the country as a whole, and actions to the contrary were un-
patriotic. Franco and many of his colleagues may have had good
reason to resist the political pressures of the *Juntas*, whose fight
for their own professional advantages was not especially helpful
to the Spaniards who were risking their lives in the name of national interest. But at least some professional egotism also shaped
his definition of patriotism and national interest.

For Franco, the *Juntas* represented all the negative aspects of
politics. Significantly, he wrote in the 1930s that the *Juntas* had
helped set the stage for the disaster of Annual, and he then associated them with the Second Republic, which he feared might
face another military disaster in Morocco. In the case of the *Juntas* and then the Republic during the early 1930s, he saw intervention by civilian politicians in military matters as inherently
detrimental to the army's mission, and thus by extension to
Spain as a whole. It is clear, moreover, that Franco's views resembled those of many other officers. Gen. Emilio Mola Vidal, who
planned the military rebellion that sparked the civil war, quoted
Franco's article on the Republic's Moroccan policies at length in
a book he published in 1934.[14]

In the early 1920s, however, Franco usually avoided interfer-
ing openly in civilian government. When the public debate
about merit promotions refused to abate, he took a more prudent route and avoided Millán-Astray's very public anti-*juntero*
campaign. In fact, when Millán-Astray finally went so far that
the government took away his command of the Legion, Franco
hoped to succeed him. But Franco lacked sufficient rank. General Sanjurjo had recommended his promotion to lieutenant
colonel after the recapture of Nador, but that recommendation
had been rejected. Thus Franco was still only a major, which was
not sufficient for him to become the new head of the Legion.

Unable to become commander of the Legion, he requested a
posting on the Spanish peninsula and subsequently reassumed

the position of head of the prince's regiment in Oviedo. But it did not take long for him to return to Africa. In early June 1923 the man chosen over him to command the Legion, Lt. Col. Rafael Valenzuela Urzaiz, died leading an attack. Shortly thereafter, Franco was promoted retroactively to lieutenant colonel and given command of the Legion.

That fall, Spain's parliamentary government was overthrown by Gen. Miguel Primo de Rivera, with considerable consequences for Franco's Moroccan endeavors. After seizing power Primo de Rivera established a dictatorship with the support of the king, and his new government's aims for the Moroccan protectorate initially alarmed Franco and other *africanistas*. With time, those aims would change more to Franco's liking, and the dictator would even give him a choice posting as the director of an important new military academy.

In the meantime, though, Primo de Rivera's talk of abandoning Morocco horrified Franco. To him, talk of abandoning the place where he had fought so hard and so many Spaniards had lost their lives was practically tantamount to treason. Now he was more than willing, moreover, to use the influence he wielded among other officers and in sections of the Spanish public to strengthen his case.

Within the military community, he voiced his opinion in the pages of a journal he helped found in North Africa, the *Revista de Tropas Coloniales*. Among the civilian public, he was already benefiting from the very laudatory press coverage of his October 1923 marriage. His best man had been none other than King Alfonso XIII, represented by proxy by the local military governor. With this kind of support, Franco was someone whom even a dictator could not easily dismiss.

During a tour of the protectorate's Spanish zone, Franco personally urged Primo de Rivera to maintain a full commitment to the Moroccan war, an opinion he made especially clear during a banquet in the dictator's honor. Although Franco's behavior was probably not as insulting and insubordinate as many later claimed, he delivered a speech in front of the dictator explicitly condemning the idea of a Spanish withdrawal. Not only had too much Spanish blood been shed, he argued, but Spain was now closer than ever to gaining complete control over the zone.

Believing otherwise, shortly after the banquet Primo de Rivera ordered the withdrawal of Spanish forces from much of the zone's interior. For the Spaniards who saw only grief in their country's North African adventures, the move was a welcome step toward what they hoped would be complete abandonment in the future. For Spaniards like Franco, on the other hand, the withdrawal was extremely painful. And not surprisingly, the move greatly facilitated Abd al-Karim al-Khattabi's own military ambitions and bolstered the morale of his troops. Many Moroccans became so optimistic that they believed the British government to have recognized Abd al-Karim's cause.[15]

Primo de Rivera's plan called for the abandonment of the more isolated and vulnerable outposts in the interior, thereby moving large numbers of troops to safer towns such as Ceuta, Larache, and Tetuan. Such a withdrawal had the advantage of shortening communication lines and allowing for greater force concentrations, but it also entailed pulling out of more than 400 forward outposts and several towns that some officers felt very guilty about leaving. Not unlike the sentiments of the South Vietnamese in 1973 with whom the Americans had sided, the Moroccans who had cooperated with the occupying Spaniards felt betrayed.

This feeling was especially strong in Chauen, where the Jewish community and others who had collaborated with the Spaniards had to abandon the town and almost surely then suffered further violence.[16] In his recollections of the Spanish withdrawal from Chauen, Franco wrote a dramatic account of the extremely negative reaction of the townspeople, with their "saddened and fearful eyes." He described the many residents of Chauen who had benefited from the Spanish occupation but now had to join the departing Spanish caravans for fear of the "fanatical reaction" they would otherwise face from returning anti-Spanish Moroccans.[17]

Yet from a more technical military perspective, the Spanish withdrawals of 1924 revealed that the Spanish military had made notable improvements, and Franco and the Legion played a prominent role in many of these operations. The Spaniards had important technological advantages that they did not hesitate to employ, including chemical weapons and air power. But their success also demonstrated a growing understanding of combined-arms warfare and the operational level of war in general.

Franco and Mola were the immediate subordinates to Gen. Julián Serrano Orive during the first phase of the Spanish withdrawal and fight from Chauen back to Tetuan. General Serrano was probably one of Spain's best generals at the time, providing Franco with a valuable learning experience. But the route to Tetuan was not an easy one, and during the last week in August, Franco fought hard battles that resulted in more than one hundred Legion casualties.

The siege of an encircled Spanish position at Solano provided Franco with an especially bitter learning experience. Although the trapped Spaniards held out for several days, in the end the Legion failed to break the siege and even had to pull back to prevent their own encirclement by the enemy. The Rifians then overran the position, killing most of its defenders. Franco and General Serrano were both strongly affected by the events at Solano, which Franco feared might foreshadow another military disaster along the lines of Annoual. During the civil war, Franco's memories of the Chauen withdrawal may have combined with his innate pride and obstinate nature to strengthen his ongoing refusal to yield any territory whatsoever to the Republicans. In the meantime, Franco's disgust with Primo de Rivera's policy may have even led him briefly to consider taking part in a coup against the dictator, although he soon abandoned this idea.[18]

In late September General Castro Girona's column began an attack to open up the road to Chauen, with the intention of evacuating the city itself. As part of this column, Franco commanded the Legion's first and third *banderas*. Thanks to Abd al-

Karim's decision to move troops to the area in hopes of causing another Spanish disaster like that of Annual, the withdrawal was a very risky operation. As in the fighting that had taken place throughout the month, Franco lost soldiers and officers— even if in the end his forces killed more of the enemy. The Legion's task was to fight the enemy directly and at the same time occupy important positions from which the retreating Spanish convoy might come under attack. The *banderas* under Franco's command took part in various operations, some very bloody, through early December 1924. The evacuation of Chauen itself was especially noteworthy.

On 15 November Castro Girona led most of the troops silently out of the city. He had already negotiated with Chauen notables and, through them, Abd al-Karim's representatives for a peaceful withdrawal and pledge of no reprisals against Chauen's residents once the Spaniards left. Although Spanish pilots who knew nothing of the negotiations bombed the nearby town where the meeting between Abd al-Karim's representatives and the notables took place, Castro Girona's endeavors were nevertheless successful. Legionnaires under Franco's command first stayed behind as the rearguard, finally leaving the city themselves on the night of 18 November. To facilitate their retreat, they left straw-filled dummies in legionnaire dress behind. The deception worked until daybreak, when Abd al-Karim's forces saw what had happened. They immediately attacked, attempting to cut off the retreating Spaniards, but by now most of the evacuation columns had a sufficient head start.

In a sense, the withdrawal of more than 40,000 men from Chauen to Tetuan was a success. Making ample use of mustard gas, high explosives, and incendiary bombs, the Spanish forces in Morocco revealed that they had made significant operational and organizational improvements. Although Franco himself probably does not deserve much credit for the operation's success beyond the tactical level of the units he commanded, it provided him and many other officers with valuable lessons with a fighting force that was far more efficient than the army he had joined in Morocco more than a decade earlier.

But Spain paid a high cost for the withdrawal. Although it is difficult to arrive at a precise number, the campaign's toll may have resulted in many more than 10,000 casualties. Moreover, Abd al-Karim's forces remained a very real threat to the Spaniards, having advanced to the gates of Ceuta and within artillery range of Tetuan. They also cut communication lines between those two cities and Tangier. In addition, the Rifians soon began to threaten French interests to the south. Yet their very successes eventually provoked their downfall. In response to the growing threat posed by the Rifians, Primo de Rivera and French military leadership began to cooperate and consider more drastic measures, including an unprecedented but previously planned amphibious landing in Al Hoceima Bay. The operation involved ground, air, and naval forces from two European countries and indigenous North African units, all working together according to careful plans.[19]

Before all these elements came together, however, in January 1925, Franco and his colleagues had the chance to practice some of the relevant tactics in a much smaller amphibious operation at Alcazarseguer on the Anjera coast, where a rebellion posed a threat to the Spanish rearguard. After two reconnoitering trips on Spanish gunboats, Franco made plans for the Anjera landing, but rough seas forced the operation's cancellation.

The Spaniards attempted the amphibious landing again in March, this time with more success. After the Spanish navy and air force bombed and strafed the coastal villages, "K"-landing barges carried Franco and the troops to the shore, where they took control of the port and defeated the Anjera rebels. These same boats had seen action in an earlier, disastrous but much-better remembered amphibious operation during World War I at Gallipoli in 1915–16. The Spaniards had later purchased the "K"-landing craft in Gibraltar, and in North Africa the boats met with much more success than they had in the Dardanelles. The Anjera operation, which took place under the overall command of Gen. Federico de Sousa Regoyos, afforded Franco firsthand experience in combined arms and amphibious warfare. In early September this experience proved especially valuable in Al Hoceima Bay.

Franco himself did not conceive of or lead the planning of the Al Hoceima operation. In fact, the idea of an amphibious landing there dated back at least to 1909, and the operation that finally took place in 1925 was the product of Primo de Rivera and some of his leading generals, especially Sanjurjo. But Franco was not entirely divorced from the planning either, and he figured prominently in the actual execution of the operation. In many ways, moreover, the operation foreshadowed the kind of combined-arms coordination that his side came closest to mastering in the Spanish Civil War.

Basing their plans in part on the lessons they gleaned from Gallipoli, the planners of the Al Hoceima invasion endeavored not only to link together various mutually supporting forces in the bay itself, but they also tried to strategically coordinate their operations with a French move northward from France's zone in the south. After the French gained control of the southern theater and the Spanish ground forces had seized the bay, the Rifians were meant to find themselves trapped in a gradually closing pincer.

Preparations for the invasion began in early June, and they came to include special training for machine gunners and artillerymen, endurance exercises, and practice landings on beaches near Ceuta and Melilla. All three branches of the Spanish military took part in the tactical planning of the invasion, in which land forces of two brigades—each with about 9,000 men—were to play a central role. On the water the Spanish forces included two battleships, four cruisers, two destroyers, eight torpedo boats, six gunboats, eleven armed trawlers, one seaplane tender, two tugs, ten transports, three hospital ships, a water tender (with another in reserve), and twenty-six landing barges, including the Gallipoli-era "K"-barges that the Spaniards had used in March on the Anjera coast. The French contribution included a battleship, two cruisers, two destroyers, two monitors, and one tug with a barrage balloon.

Inevitably, the carefully-planned Al Hoceima invasion suffered various hitches in its execution. Uncooperative weather and strong currents delayed the actual start of the landings by one day to 8 September, which meant that columns of soldiers had to spend forty-eight hours packed into rocking and pitching boats. Unexpected rocks and shoals stopped the landing barges fifty meters from the shoreline, thereby rendering useless the ten Renault FT-17 light tanks that were supposed to precede and support the landing. In fact, when the high command became aware of this problem, it tried to cancel the invasion. But Franco disobeyed this command, ordering his men to join him in jumping overboard. Under fire and holding their guns and munitions above their heads, they waded to the beach.

Franco later wrote a very colorful account of his role in the Al Hoceima invasion, noteworthy as much for its style as for its content. With its emotional and descriptive prose, it went far beyond a dry military report. Instead, Franco clearly intended to fascinate and impress:

> The black barges, with their raised bows and their strange, primitive appearance, crash through the sea froth. Their motors, together with those of the tugs, make an infernal noise. The canon fire thunders over our heads and the black smoke of the naval artillery's explosions engulfs the coast. The enemy's cannon and machine-gun fire passes over our heads, as he tries to halt our advance. We reach a few thousand meters from the shore; the tugs cut loose and the buckling barges [*panzudas barcazas*], impelled by their own motors, carry their impassioned human cargos toward the cursed land. Our fate has been cast! These are moments of extreme emotions.[20]

In spite of Franco's description, though, a combination of superior resources, coordination, and luck were more important to the eventual Spanish success at Al Hoceima than individual bravery in the face of the danger. Seventy-six aircraft bombarded the surrounding area with traditional explosives and mustard gas before the Spanish landing began. At sea, the Spanish and French navies also bombarded Abd al-Karim's positions, using an observation balloon for more accurate targeting. Abd al-

Karim had received intelligence about the coming invasion, but he may have been caught off guard when the Spaniards came ashore by accident at the wrong beaches. Similar to the manner in which the inadvertent scattering of American paratroopers would confuse the German defenders on World War II's D-Day, some of the errors at Al Hoceima actually proved helpful to the Spaniards, steering them away from better-defended areas.

Yet even if aspects of its planning were flawed and the operation did not always unfold smoothly, the invasion did not betray what one historian inaccurately terms "the appalling organization of the Spanish Army" either.[21] Overall, the operation was a success, greatly benefiting Spanish as well as French strategic interests. Within the Spanish armed forces, coordination between the infantry, air force, and artillery had made significant gains, and military effectiveness in general had clearly improved. Even the French, who had scorned earlier Spanish military endeavors in the protectorate, now had some good words for the Spaniards.

France's own recent setbacks in the protectorate had also helped change their opinion of the Spaniards, as they now knew from firsthand experience that the Rifians were formidable opponents. But the Al Hoceima operation in itself also earned French praise, even if at the same time the French criticized its commanding officer, General Sanjurjo, and some aspects of its implementation. According to a French liaison officer writing to Marshall Philippe Pétain about the Spanish forces after witnessing the invasion, "A great enterprise of organization and training has been accomplished and the first impression I have of this army is that it is a solid and perfectly tested instrument."[22]

Franco was not the chief architect of the Al Hoceima landings. But on a hitherto unprecedented scale, the amphibious invasion made clear to him the importance of operational planning and execution. He also saw firsthand how important it was to make use of highly competent and intelligent officers from different branches of service in the operations themselves, and the invasion especially reinforced his appreciation of the artillery. As an infantryman, he could easily have shared the profound hatred of many of his colleagues for the artillery corps, with its aristocratic character and very different political interests. But Franco continued to stress the importance of the artillery and praise its officers in his writings. And after the civil war broke out in 1936, he revealed that his words were anything but hollow, appointing artillerymen like Carlos Martínez de Campos to powerful and important staff positions. These appointments did not stem solely from necessity; as a young officer in Morocco, Franco had been one of the few men within the infantry to go out of his way to praise the artillery and its importance in the fighting.

For his role in the Al Hoceima landing, Franco received enough merit points to advance to the rank of brigadier general on 3 February 1926. On the very night he was promoted, members of his class at the Infantry Academy feted him, since he was the first cadet of their year to reach the rank of general. At the same time, his brother Ramón brought even more public acclaim to the family by making an unprecedented transatlantic flight to South America. Even though Ramón received more attention in a public celebration in their hometown of El Ferrol several days later, Franco certainly did not disappear from the spotlight. On a personal level, 1926 was also an important year for him; his only child, María de Carmen, was born on 14 September 1926. Probably not coincidentally, his days of personally leading his men in battle were now behind him.

In early 1928 Primo de Rivera made Franco head of the newly reestablished *Academia General Militar*. Although the position gave Franco even more public attention, he characteristically clung to his traditional military identity and denied any interest in politics. When a journalist asked him in 1928 if he now considered himself a politician, his curt reply was, "I'm a soldier [*militar*]."[23]

Franco's directorship of this new academy was significant in several ways. First, the philosophy behind the reopening of the *Academia General* was in itself a good match for Franco, since it was intended to help overcome the ingrained separation between the infantry, artillery, and other corps of the army. Army cadets would now spend their first two years at the *Academia General* before pursuing more specialized studies in their separate academies.

As we have seen, in Morocco Franco had come to appreciate the practical reasons to foster better relations within the army, especially between the infantry and the artillery, and he had even gone to some lengths to praise the artillery in his published writings. Many other infantry officers, on the other hand, had not found it so easy to overcome their interservice prejudices. The opposition to the reestablishment of the *Academia General* by one of the infantry's leading military educators and textbook authors, Enrique Ruiz-Fornells, was telling. Ruiz-Fornells, who had already made his profound dislike of the artillery corps clear, strongly opposed the reestablishment of the *Academia General*, which he feared might prove a threat to the infantry's relative position within the armed forces. Although other reasons, including a personal dislike of Franco himself, also influenced Ruiz-Fornells and other military opponents of the new academy, interservice rivalry definitely colored their views.

The general characteristics of the academy's professors also revealed much about Franco's views of war and military education. He chose fellow *africanistas* like himself, who could imbue the cadets with conservative, imperialist nationalist values and at the same time impart upon them the practical lessons of combat in Morocco. In fact, Franco seems to have rejected the traditional system of military textbooks altogether, preferring instead a more hands-on approach to education. This decision by Franco undoubtedly reflected in part his own academic and intellectual shortcomings, and the academy professors' emphasis on willpower, bravery, and right-wing nationalism instead of more rationalist, scientific, and theoretical aspects of war undoubtedly left its mark on the cadets—as Franco intended. His own brother, Ramón, complained about the "troglodytic education" imparted by the academy's conservative professors, although the politically radical Ramón was not exactly an impartial critic. But some of Franco's decisions as academy director clearly did not stem from an anti-intellectual outlook.

His refusal to base the curriculum around textbooks, for instance, was a rational response to a significant and deeply entrenched problem in Spanish military education. The long-time professors at Spanish military academies often supplemented their incomes by writing new, and often superfluous, editions of military textbooks. It was not just Franco who disliked this practice; other officers also found it appalling. Franco, however, went beyond mere protests and took concrete actions against what one officer had called the "blind mercantilism" behind the institution of military textbook publishing.[24]

In the end, then, Franco found a comfortable and prominent position for himself in the dictatorship of Primo de Rivera, with whom he had initially clashed over Morocco. He also liked much about the Primo de Rivera regime in general, especially the way it had apparently overcome many of the problems that he believed parliamentary politics had wrought upon Spain. In fact, Franco emulated many aspects of Primo de Rivera's system of rule when he began to establish his own dictatorship during the civil war. In the meantime, though, the situation did not remain so much to his liking.

By the late 1920s Primo de Rivera lost much of his early support, and in late January 1930 he stepped down. After two other military figures unsuccessfully tried their hand at ruling the country alongside the king, the Spanish monarchy itself began to falter. The king no longer enjoyed the support he had once taken for granted, whether in the throne as part of a parliamentary monarchy or with a military dictatorship. After the monarchy itself fell in April 1931, the stage was set for the establishment of Spain's first democracy. For Franco, this period marked one of Spanish history's lowest points. Ironically, though, in the end the first democracy made possible his rise from the esteemed position as a soldier that he had already achieved to the position of supreme commander and dictator.

Chapter 4

From Reluctant Rebel to Generalísimo

T HE 1930S constituted the most decisive period in Franco's life, both as a soldier and as a political figure. Not only Franco found these years so crucial; the period had long-lasting effects in much of the world. In Spain, however, the conflicting political, social, and military forces converged in an especially violent and spectacular fashion.

As a result, Franco became the major figure in a war involving, besides virtually all Spaniards in one way or another, the armed forces of Hitler's Germany, Mussolini's Italy, and Stalin's Soviet Union. The conflict became known by some as a training ground for World War II, but it grew out of conditions in Spain itself, which had evolved so much to the dislike of Franco that he would join other generals in attempting to overthrow the government by force. Their actions encountered more resistance than they expected, sparking the Spanish Civil War (1936–1939).

Even before the civil war and its many complications took the world stage, the situation in Spain was extremely complex. During the first part of the 1930s, Spain saw the fall of its monarchy, its first democracy, a major revolutionary insurrection, an attempted military coup, growing street violence, and an array of evolving political parties and coalitions. In the meantime, Spaniards felt the international climate heat up as Hitler rose to power, communism remained a force to be reckoned with, and major economic depression plagued much of the world. Because a full description to the background to the civil war is not possible here, this chapter will focus on the major events leading up to the war and the developments most relevant to Franco's rise to supreme commander and then dictator.

April 1931 saw the establishment of Spain's first democracy, the Second Republic. (The First Republic had existed very briefly more than a half century earlier.) It came into being after public support for the monarchy reached an all-time low. Spanish Republicans, who had long dreamed of abolishing the monarchy, finally got their chance after the municipal elections that took place all over Spain on 12 April 1931. Overall, the anti-monarchists did very well in these elections, and their success made it clear how many people were ready for a change. To make matters worse for the king, key military leaders gave up on the monarchy and made it clear that they would no longer support it. As a result, King Alfonso XIII abandoned the government. But as was the case in many European countries between the world wars, democracy in Spain did not last long. Only after Franco's death in 1975 did Spain see it again.

Yet at the time of its founding, the Second Republic certainly did not appear doomed. Many Spaniards, including some leading army officers and generals, had high hopes for the new government. As a man with much respect for tradition, Franco was undoubtedly saddened by the death of the monarchy. He had benefited personally from the intervention of the king on behalf of his own promotion years earlier. During a small, unsuccessful Republican revolt in December 1930, Franco had gone as far as to mobilize the cadets of the *Academia General Militar* to block a major road in defense of the monarchy.[1] Nevertheless, his reaction to the proclamation of the Republic was muted, even though a few developments that accompanied it were cause for concern.

The Republic was Spain's first government to officially separate church and state, and those who disliked the Catholic Church, with its extensive political and social power, were very pleased to see this traditionally anti-modern and conservative bastion lose its privileged position. But extremists went as far as to celebrate by setting fire to churches all over Spain, making it painfully clear how much some Spaniards hated the church and its power. Franco's own brother, Ramón, the famous pilot with a disposition for radical politics, participated in the violence. Ramón, expressing an extreme but not unique point of view, later remarked that he had "contemplated with joy those magnificent flames as the expression of a people who wanted to free itself from clerical obscurantism."[2]

The failure of the new government's security forces to act against these violent, sacrilegious acts dismayed Franco and many other Spaniards, who feared they might signal things to come. In fact, some leading politicians who supported the new Republic, themselves practicing Catholics, were equally upset. But in general the governmental response to the anti-clerical violence was weak, and the widely disseminated images of governmental indifference to the church burnings only reinforced the opposition of many practicing Catholics to the Republic.

Another development that troubled Franco during the Second Republic was the rise of the extreme political left. During the 1920s he had begun to read anticommunist literature, and as a result communism began to occupy a place similar to that of Freemasonry in his mind. Communism was not a strong political force in Spain until the outbreak of the civil war; the most successful political groups of the extreme left were anarchists. But Franco became obsessed with the idea of a communist—and a Masonic—conspiracy during the 1930s, when it had apparently become clear that the Russian Revolution was not going to be reversed.[3]

On a more personal and immediate level, the new Republican government affected Franco the most with its reforms of the Spanish military, which were intended to reduce its excess of officers and modernize the armed forces in general. The man behind the reforms, the Left Republican and War Minister Manuel Azaña, was a very controversial figure whom many officers soon came to hate. In fact, Azaña's image in the military world may not have been damaged as much by the measures he took to reform the armed forces as by his arrogant attitude and disdain for military professionals, among others. Even some leftist supporters of the Republic condemned Azaña's attitude and lack of sympathy for those with other views.[4] Azaña also served as an easy target for the right-wing press, which quoted him as making particularly strong negative statements about the military, some of which he had never made. In other words, his judgment and remarks as a public figure were not always particularly helpful to the Republic, especially with regard to military affairs, and his right-wing enemies did their best to make the situation even worse.

As the monarchist officer Carlos Martínez de Campos later observed, however, in many ways the "nervousness" caused by Azaña's reform decree was "greater than its material effects." The Spanish army may have desperately needed major reforms, but it was impossible to reform an institution like the army without upsetting some of its members, each of whom naturally favored—as Martínez de Campos noted—criteria most suitable to his own interests. Nevertheless, in the monarchist's view "the bad moments were brief" during the process of military reform, and the armed forces clearly needed drastic changes.[5]

The "bad moments" may have been brief, but their effects were occasionally profound, and in the opinion of some other leading military figures, they were not so easy to forget or forgive. The reforms provoked the subsequent planner of the military rebellion that sparked the civil war, Gen. Emilio Mola Vidal, to write a book in protest, arguing that they created more problems than they solved.[6] Franco also had good reason to dislike the reforms. In one of Azaña's first major decisions as war minister, which went into effect when the Republic was less than three months old, he closed the *Academia General Militar*, causing Franco to lose a position that he valued greatly.

Franco made his sentiments clear in his farewell speech on the academy parade ground in July 1931, although his message seemed to contradict itself at times. On the one hand, he urged cadets to retain their discipline and follow orders from above even when they thought them to be wrong. But on the other hand, he failed to show much self-discipline himself, making it clear that he personally disliked the Republic and viewed the officers serving in the new government as "pernicious." In other words, the loyalty and discipline he demanded from cadets was directed at the fatherland in general and the institution he viewed as its best representative: the army. In his view, the current national government was not the same as the Spanish nation. Such thinking served to justify the rebellion that sparked the civil war, which Franco interpreted as an act of patriotism. More immediately, the speech earned Franco an official reprimand from Azaña.[7]

Another consequence of the military reforms was the lowering of Franco's place on the top-heavy Spanish army's seniority list, although he was allowed to keep his rank as a brigadier general and he received a new assignment soon thereafter. His new posting was in La Coruña, the major city in Galicia, where he commanded the infantry garrison. But he was not completely removed from national politics, and he knew that many fellow officers had already lost hope in the civilian politicians.

In 1932 Franco himself received an offer to join other officers who were planning to overthrow the Republic, but he turned them down. As he correctly predicted, the ill-planned coup attempt failed anyway. In part because he now appeared to be one of the more loyal generals, the government rewarded him with a choice posting in February 1933: commander of the Balearic Islands district. During this period his interests remained primarily in military affairs, and he avoided implicating himself in political conspiracies. After meeting with Franco, the former government minister Natalio Rivas reported that the Republic could count on the general's continuing support, even if Franco had concerns about recent developments in Morocco.

Yet at the same time Franco began to gain the attention of some influential members of the political right. During the late 1920s, he had begun to assume the identity not just of a military hero but also of someone well respected within the political establishment. Nevertheless, he continued to resist becoming directly involved in the world of Spanish politics. Because he also refused to commit himself to the schemes of fellow officers against the national government, the ever-prudent Franco still did not have a very precise political identity when the Republic entered into serious crisis. He did not associate himself with the left, but to many moderate Republicans he did not seem far enough to the right to pose a threat either.[8]

On a professional level Franco had an obvious interest in the success of more conservative political elements. His fortunes rose when a coalition of moderate and right-wing parties, including the conservative alliance CEDA (*Confederación Española de Derechas Autónomas*), triumphed in the November elections. An important CEDA delegate was Ramón Serrano Súñer, Franco's brother-in-law who later played a key role in his dictatorship. In addition to this tie to CEDA, Franco was well regarded by leaders of the Radical Party, which—in spite of its name—was a moderate Republican party. The Radicals led the governing coalition, which meant they held the cabinet position of the Ministry of War, among others. CEDA, on the other hand, was still kept out of the government, even though it had received the most votes in the last election. In March 1934 War Minister Diego Hidalgo, a Radical, promoted Franco to major general (*general de división*).

Yet even if Franco's fortunes in the Republic had improved, Spain as a whole was not faring as well. Many Spaniards continued to suffer severe economic hardships, and the political scene became increasingly polarized—often violently so. The Socialist leader Francisco Largo Caballero spoke ever more of revolution and openly praised the Soviet Union, frightening many members of the middle and upper classes. At the same time, to many Spaniards, the CEDA leader José María Gil Robles appeared strikingly similar to Hitler and Mussolini at times, and the anti-Republican attitudes of many conservatives only seemed to harden with time. On the international scene Hitler had recently used his position within Germany's parliamentary government to establish a dictatorship and crush the socialists. Many Spanish socialists and others feared the same fate might befall them in Spain.

Thus the naming of three CEDA members to parliamentary positions in 1934 appeared to them as the first step toward the establishment of a dictatorship in Spain, even though CEDA had earned its right to govern in free and democratic elections. The result was a general strike, a declaration of independence by the regional Catalan government, and an attempted revolution in the coal-mining area of Asturias, where anarchists and socialists teamed up. Even if in hindsight this so-called October Revolution never really threatened the existence of the central government itself, Franco saw it as "the first step towards the implantation of communism in our nation," and he was certainly not alone in his fear. The Spanish Second Republic had already suffered from much revolutionary violence, including three anarchist insurrections in 1932–33. But this time the revolutionary uprising was even larger—possibly the largest in modern west European history up to that point.[9]

After the revolt broke out on 5 October, Franco became a special technical advisor to the Ministry of War, charged with coordinating the military response and suppression of the uprising in Asturias. The move resulted in part from resistance in some circles to sending in Franco as the field commander, as the war minister and some leading conservatives wanted. The war minister, having just made Franco his personal technical advisor for the army maneuvers of late September, may have already decided to use Franco in the event of an insurrection.[10] In any case, naming Franco to the special advisory position in the War Ministry made sense from a purely technical perspective. He was, after all, a proven operational-level commander, having displayed a high interest in the careful planning and coordination of military actions since his days as a young officer in Morocco.

At this point the War Ministry's Operations Section was still a rather lethargic institution, dedicated more to long-term strategic matters than immediate, operational questions of time, space, and coordination. When Franco arrived at the ministry, he discovered serious deficiencies in intelligence, communications, organization, and other fundamental aspects of operations. The Operations Section thus lacked the capability to respond to ever-changing events as rapidly as Franco wanted. But after Franco's arrival the priorities of the section quickly shifted from long-term strategy to the immediate and instantaneous coordination of communications, analysis, and organization—in other words, to the operational level of war.[11]

During the insurrection itself Franco's unofficial operations staff was small but effective. It was manned by Franco himself, his cousin Francisco "Pacón" Franco Salgado-Araujo, and two naval officers. Housed in the War Ministry's telegraph room, this multi-service command unit directed combined operations against the Asturian "enemies" for two weeks. Franco and his assistants coordinated troop and supply movements by ground, air, and sea, artillery bombardments from ships, attacks from the air, and the use of railroads. Under Franco's direction, the military response to the events of October 1934 in Asturias achieved its goals, although some 1,000 revolutionaries and more than 400 members of the army and police forces lost their lives. Franco also brought in units of the Spanish Foreign Legion and the Moroccan *Regulares*.

To his critics, Franco's use of the Moroccans seemed to have symbolic meaning, since Asturias was known as the only part of Spain not conquered by Arabs during the Middle Ages. But Franco was probably less interested in symbols than in practical concerns; even the left Republican leader Azaña had called upon the Legion and the *Regulares* to squash an anarchist insurrection two years earlier. By using experienced Moroccan units, Franco could also assuage his fears that Spanish troops might not act as

decisively as he wanted against fellow Spaniards like the Asturi-
ans. In the paternalistic colonial vision he shared with many
africanistas, the Moroccan troops—although Muslims and thus
the historic enemies of Christian Spain—had a higher place in
the social hierarchy than Marxist and anarchist workers. In his
eyes, the Asturian campaign constituted "a frontier war against
socialism, communism and whatever attacks civilization in order
to replace it with barbarism."[12] Franco thus expected the military
forces in Asturias to act as forcefully with the miners as they
would against external enemies. He removed from the campaign
officers who he thought might sympathize with the miners, including his own cousin and childhood companion, Air Force
Major Ricardo de la Puente Bahamonde.

Because the Asturian uprising soon became an important
symbol for both the Right and the Left, subsequent propaganda
makes it difficult to discern the degree of bloodshed and atrocities with complete accuracy. Still, it seems clear that the military
and police acted with considerable and unnecessary brutality at
times, with at least one of the commanders in the field ordering
summary executions. After the miners surrendered, army and
civil guard units conducted thorough and often violent sweeps
to ensure that absolutely no resistance remained, and hundreds
of prisoners were beaten and tortured.

The failed revolution of 1934 had a major impact on Spanish
politics. Franco, however, remained outwardly apolitical. As
long as the conservative government remained in power, he saw
no reason to accept offers to join any military conspiracy against
the Republic. Censorship, judicial rulings, and many aspects of
the current government's policy worked against the leftists who
Franco so disliked. Besides, he was too cautious to commit himself to a conspiracy that he was not sure would succeed.

In February 1936, however, the Popular Front, a coalition including Socialists, Communists, Republicans, and others, won
the national elections. In the view of fearful conservatives, Spain
was now lurching once again toward a disastrous revolution.
Still, Franco hesitated to participate in the plans of some of his

colleagues and right-wing politicians to use force to stop the Republic's slide to the left. At the same time, he was visibly disturbed when large crowds of people took to the streets to celebrate the election results.

Fearing that the election celebration would get out of hand, he urged the declaration of martial law and the calling out of troops, an act that some have interpreted as a move toward a coup d'état. But such a declaration would not have constituted a complete rejection of the Republic; in fact, Franco was trying to quell the perceived leftist threat without breaking completely with the bounds of legality. Even the progressive government of the Second Republic had demonstrated a willingness to use force against some leftist insurrections, and Franco feared that the post-election crowds might soon become violent and pose a significant threat. Thus while he may have been rather paranoid, his willingness to call out troops and effect the same kind of "police action" he had employed in Asturias was not equivalent to an attempted coup.[13]

Yet Franco was plainly displeased with the election results, as Azaña, who was now prime minister, was well aware. Hence Azaña assigned Franco to the military command of the Canary Islands off the northwest coast of Africa. By so doing, Azaña hoped to distance him from possible conspiracies in Madrid. He also wanted to ensure that Franco was not in charge of a substantial garrison capable of participating in an insurrection, such as one in mainland Spain or Morocco.

Franco was now a very public figure, and many leftists viewed his role in the suppression of the Asturian uprising as unforgivable. When he arrived in the Canary Islands, he saw graffiti calling for his death, and he soon felt the need for twenty-four-hour guard for himself and his family. To make matters worse for him, the Popular Front government that was now in power had not only amnestied the revolutionaries imprisoned after the 1934 uprising, but it was also beginning to prosecute those involved in its suppression. In the view of many Popular Front leaders, the uprising sparked by the 1934 elections was an understandable reaction to realistic fears of a fascist takeover, like those that had brought Hitler and Mussolini to power. But in the eyes of conservatives like Franco, 1934 had made clear the hypocrisy of the leftists, who seemed to support the Republic and its constitution only when things went their way.

In order to protect Franco from possible prosecution for his role in the Asturias suppression, right-wing politicians suggested putting him on their list of candidates for the town of Cuenca in a special parliamentary by-election in May. They reasoned that with a seat in parliament, Franco could claim parliamentary immunity. But José Antonio Primo de Rivera, the son of the late dictator and leader of the Spanish Fascist Party, the *Falange*, rejected this idea. José Antonio had met Franco only once, and during their meeting Franco's unwillingness to take a stand and commit himself to a firm position had frustrated the Fascist leader. Franco's lack of experience in politics and questionable public speaking skills had also made José Antonio wary. Furthermore, he feared that including Franco on the list would make it appear even more right-wing than he wanted, given Franco's reputation as a very conservative military figure.

In the meantime, the social and political situation in Spain continued to deteriorate. Political strife akin to that in Germany before Hitler's dictatorship and in France between the world wars was becoming ever more violent. Ideological inflexibility, extremist discourse, economic hardship, and a refusal to compromise made governing Spain increasingly difficult. Middle-of-the-road politics lost out to extremes on the right and the left. Political assassinations became more frequent, as hit men and death squads meted out their deadly violence.

Between the February elections and the outbreak of the civil war in mid-July, this violence yielded 269 deaths and more than 1,200 wounded. Life during this period was further disrupted by 113 strikes and more than 225 partial shutdowns. Under the Popular Front, Spain also saw its justice system grow increasingly politicized in favor of the Left. The seizure of the church and other lands and the closing of Catholic schools were among the developments that deeply disturbed many Spaniards on the Right. With these conditions as a backdrop, even the ever-cautious Franco finally agreed to participate in an attempt by other military officers to take over the country.

But his transformation into an active conspirator against the Republic was slow—maddeningly so for some of the other generals. Franco did not meet for the first time with the generals conspiring against the Popular Front until early March 1936. Even then he still did not appear completely committed; Gen. Emilio Mola, the organizer and chief planner of the military revolt, had doubts about Franco's commitment until the very last moment.

Mola's plans for a new government in Spain were not very precise or extensive. The generals who rose up on the night of 17–18 July, thereby sparking the Spanish Civil War, were a relatively diverse bunch. Gen. José Enrique Varela, for instance, wanted to abrogate the constitution, suppress all the parties of the Left, establish state control of the press, and unify all the right-wing parties into a single force. Mola and others, on the other hand, wanted to preserve some form of Republican government in Spain. Their aim was not a democratic republic of the kind they believed was now failing so miserably in Spain, but it was not truly fascist or a complete rejection of liberal parliamentary principles either. In any case, the program Mola drew up was vague and really more of a rough sketch than anything else, and no one took it very seriously.

What united the conspirators was their desire to bring an end through military means to what seemed like a dangerous, revolutionary situation that was spiraling out of control, threatening themselves and other conservative forces in Spain. Some of the civilians who allied with these generals may have had more radical, or even fascist, ideas, but most of the generals wanted only to effect what they saw as a large-scale police action, restoring law and order to Spain. Most did not give too much thought to precisely what would happen beyond vague ideas of authoritarian regeneration or the strengthening of Spain's conservative status quo.

Franco himself gave even less thought than most of the other conspirators to the new regime that they would impose on Spain, and his role in the planning of the rebellion was minimal. Even after the civil war had begun, Franco's public pronouncements betrayed his lack of a clear political ideology. He certainly rejected more aspects of the Second Republic than some of the other conspirators, although he too claimed to be acting in the name of the Republic in his first manifesto. But even as late as July 1937, he seemed to hold somewhat contradictory and confused political goals, on some occasions espousing ultra-conservative rhetoric but on others evoking the principles of the French Revolution—albeit out of order—and claiming to act in the name of "fraternity, liberty, and equality." Initially, such ideological uncertainty proved advantageous to the Nationalists, since it allowed them to appeal to different groups at the same time.[14]

Before the war broke out, Franco's political views were even more difficult to define. After the electoral triumph of the Popular Front, he still had relatively little to say in his correspondence with Mola about the political and social conditions that led the generals to plan their coup. In fact, he continued to appear ambivalent about the coup itself.

Instead, the politically cautious Franco preferred to focus on practical military affairs. By the end of March Franco knew that his role in the planned coup d'état was to secure North Africa and then cross the Strait of Gibraltar and move northward toward Madrid with Spain's military forces in Morocco, the so-called Army of Africa. The planners expected this task to be relatively simple for Franco, with his ample prestige and experience. Nevertheless, Franco prepared for the upcoming military operation in the same careful, studious manner that he had favored since his days as a young officer in Morocco. Always a soldier, he seemed more interested in technical military affairs than in politics. He wrote to Mola in late March on the importance of tactics and terrain in military operations, stressing in a some-what didactic fashion the lessons to be found in Spanish military history.

Meanwhile, the political situation in Spain continued to deteriorate, and the inflamed rhetoric on both the Left and the Right made compromise and a working government seem ever more impossible. The increasing turmoil worked in the interests of Fascists and others of the extreme right, since it seemed to prove that democracy had failed and that Spain needed the kind of strict, authoritarian government they advocated. Politically motivated murders continued to take place on both sides of the spectrum, including the killing of a Socialist member of the Republican Assault Guards on the night of 12–13 July. This crime provided the immediate pretext for the kidnapping and murder the following night of a right-wing figure of far more political importance: opposition leader José Calvo Sotelo.

The murder of such a prominent politician was shocking in itself, but to make matters worse, Calvo Sotelo's killers were a group of left-leaning police officers working in collaboration with Socialist gunmen. An authoritarian Nationalist, Calvo Sotelo represented the face of impending fascism to many on the left, and he had made very clear his dislike of the Republic in general and his preference for regimes of the extreme political right over that of the Popular Front. But he was also a constitu-tionally elected parliamentary opposition leader. His murder at the hands of the government's own security forces was unprecedented and an outrage to many even in a country that had already seen so much political violence.

The murder provided the final impetus for Mola and his collaborators, and it probably caused Franco to overcome his hesitation and commit himself fully to the rebellion. If someone like Calvo Sotelo could be assassinated, he could be killed too. In the early afternoon of 18 July, he boarded a small private plane for Morocco. His role in the rebellion was to lead Spain's Army of Africa. He had now begun his return to mainland Spain. It took him more than two years to reach Madrid.

Chapter 5

No Mercy: Fighting the Spanish Civil War

W<small>HEN FRANCO</small> and the other military conspirators rose up against the Popular Front government in July 1936, they expected to triumph in two weeks or less. Instead, they encountered unexpectedly stiff resistance, and their actions resulted in a long and bloody war. Out of the attempted coup d'état came another unexpected consequence as well: the emergence of Francisco Franco as the overall political and military leader of the rebel forces, and then of Spain itself.

The intended leader of the rebellion, Gen. José Sanjurjo, perished in a plane crash on 20 July. Less than one year later, on 3 June 1937, the rebellion's architect, Gen. Emilio Mola, died in another plane crash. And by the end of the war Franco had effectively eliminated all possible civilian—and royal—rivals to his power. Although some observers then and now have openly wondered if the plane crashes were more than just accidents, no one has found any evidence that they were the result of deliberate sabotage. Instead, they represent yet another example of the sheer luck Franco enjoyed during his long journey from army cadet to head of state.

Yet Franco also demonstrated a considerable amount of political skill and acumen. His slow, prudent, and steady manner helped him avoid the kind of politically dangerous positions from which he could possibly experience a dramatic fall. His cautiousness also allowed him to benefit in the right conditions, although he was so careful that he did not always do so.

This cautious approach to politics had its counterpart in Franco's military thinking, as his prosecution of the civil war demonstrated. Despite what some critics have written, Franco's leadership in the war is not a textbook case of military mediocrity. Admittedly, he benefited immensely from the aid of Nazi Germany and Fascist Italy, and it is also true that he fought against an enemy suffering from severe organizational, material, and political problems.

But just as the Soviet Union's undeniable advantage of manpower and space in World War II should not blind us to their superior operational planning, the German and Italian aid during the Spanish Civil War should not obscure Franco's effectiveness as a military commander. He was not the military genius that his propagandists make him out to be, but he was not a dismal commander or military thinker either.

Upon arriving in Morocco on 18 July, Franco faced the immediate task of transporting the forces in Morocco, the Army of Africa, across the Strait of Gibraltar. This mission was made all the more important because, much to the dismay of the rebels, the military revolt had failed in several key areas. The cities of Madrid, Barcelona, Valencia, Bilbao, Oviedo, and Malaga remained in the hands of the government forces resisting the military coup, commonly referred to as the Loyalists or the Republicans. The rebel forces trying to overthrow the Republic, usually known as the Insurgents or Nationalists, had seized control or were on the verge of doing so in Burgos, Valladolid, Pamplona, Sevilla, Cádiz, Córdoba, and all of Morocco. In general terms, the Insurgents held areas in the far south, west, and northwest of Spain, but together these areas constituted only about one-third of Spanish territory. The Republicans, on the other hand, held the more industrial areas and most of the bigger cities. As had been the case when the Spanish zone of the Moroccan protectorate had been established in 1912, the forces on Franco's side needed to expand outward from separate regions.

Because sailors had foiled the actions of the naval officers wishing to join the revolt, Republican warships patrolled the Strait of Gibraltar, and Franco could not get his forces from North Africa to mainland Spain by sea. Instead, when the uprising began, he quickly sent representatives to Italy and then to Germany. The benefits of these dispatches soon became apparent. On 26 July Hitler decided to send twenty-six transport planes and other equipment, and on the following day Mussolini agreed to send twelve bombers and a small amount of other material support to the Insurgents. German and Italian planes thus joined Spanish planes that had already begun to fly Nationalist troops across the strait on 20 July. It was the first military airlift in history and it played a crucial role for the rebels during the early days of the war.

Franco's task now was to move his troops from the far south of Spain toward Madrid, as Mola moved his forces in from the north. Although Franco had only agreed to join the revolt after much hesitation, he soon became one of the most essential figures in the military revolt, thanks to his prestige and his command of the very important Army of Africa. He did not assume overall command of the Nationalist side until late September, but his importance grew considerably after the intended leader of the rebellion, General Sanjurjo, died in the 20 July plane crash.

Mola's forces made it within about twenty-five miles from the northern border of Madrid, but with no operational reserves at hand they failed to exploit their position and break through. In other words, Franco and Mola simply moved toward the city as well as they could on their own, independent of the other's progress or obstacles. Hence, Franco did not send units from the southern front to reinforce Mola when he might have achieved his breakthrough into Madrid.[1] In fact, the troops under Franco's command moved especially slowly. Part of his strategy, betraying the influence of the Annoual disaster on his thinking, consisted of gradually occupying territory, then making sure he had secured complete control and extinguishing any possible source of future resistance before moving onward. It took him more than three months to reach the outskirts of Madrid.

Along the way, the extensive Nationalist cleansing of Republican supporters not only served to eliminate the possibility of rearguard attacks but also helped to sow terror. The most extreme example of insurgent terror during the Army of Africa's march northward occurred in Badajoz and the surrounding province of the same name, located close to the Portuguese border. Under the field command of Gen. Juan Yagüe and the overall direction of Franco, the forces made a westward diversion toward the town of Badajoz, which had about 42,000 inhabitants at the time. As Franco wrote Mola on 11 August, he deemed it important to eliminate all resistance in the Nationalist-occupied areas before moving onward, even if Madrid was to remain the primary goal.[2]

On 13 August Yagüe wrote to Franco about his recent military actions and his preparations for the attack on Badajoz. Significantly, he addressed his message to the "Head of the National Government," even though Franco did not officially become head of state and supreme commander of the Nationalists until 30 September.[3] As Yagüe's word choice indicated, it was already apparent that the commander of the Army of Africa was considered by many Insurgents as their natural leader.

In Badajoz news had begun to spread of the rapes, murders, and pillaging perpetuated by the Army of Africa on its march northward, and many of the town's residents were especially terrified about what would happen should the legionnaires and Moroccan *Regulares* enter the town. Such fears undoubtedly lent impetus to the defensive measures they had already taken, including imprisoning and executing suspected Nationalist sympathizers. Like elsewhere in Spain, in Badajoz conservatives and

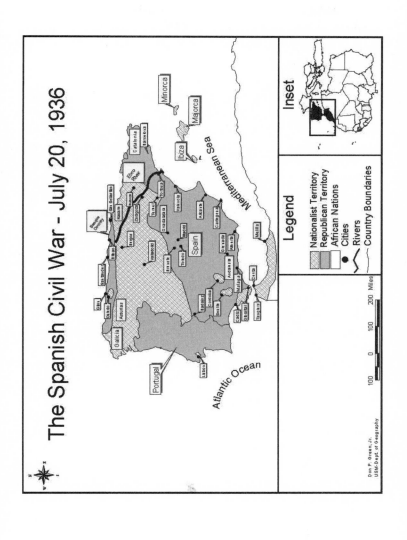

The Spanish Civil War – July 20, 1936

Legend

- Nationalist Territory
- Republican Territory
- African Nations
- Cities
- Rivers
- Country Boundaries

Inset

Portugal

Spain

Galicia

Atlantic Ocean

Mediterranean Sea

Minorca

Majorca

Ibiza

Catalonia

Ebro River

Basque Country

Don P. Green, Jr.
USM-Dept. of Geography

100   0   100   200 Miles

others thought to be against the Republic had lost their lives to leftist gunmen. In anticipation of the approaching Army of Africa, Republican militias had begun to arrive in the town to help in its defense one week before Yagüe's attack. Their improvisations yielded a surprising amount of resistance but ultimately failed to halt the attackers, who entered the town after heavy artillery and bombing attacks. A bloodbath ensued in the town, while in the entire province of Badajoz more than 6,000 people lost their lives in the repression.[4]

The massacre of Badajoz was an extreme example of the ruthlessness with which the Nationalists were capable of prosecuting the war. It exceeded by far the amount of repression that would have constituted a reasonable reaction to Republican resistance and to previous shootings of Nationalist sympathizers in the area. And in spite of Yagüe's subsequent remark that he had no choice but to eliminate a future threat to his rearguard, the rebels' military aims did not make this vast slaughter necessary. The repression did, however, correspond to Franco's more general desire throughout the war to utterly defeat the enemy and eliminate all possible future resistance in occupied areas. He did not want this war to have its equivalent to Annual.

On a much smaller scale, under Franco's orders various military figures lost their lives because they refused to rise up against the Republic. As he had done in Morocco, Franco did not hesitate to administer his version of military justice coldly and without mercy. Honorable military service in the past now counted for little; loyalty to the rebel cause was all that mattered. Among those who lost their lives to the Nationalists were Col. Domingo Batet, who suppressed the October 1934 uprising in Catalonia but years earlier had attacked Franco—at times unfairly—in an official report. Even the intervention on Batet's behalf by Cardinal Isidro Gomá y Tomás, a strong supporter of the Nationalists, failed to move Franco.[5]

Franco also ordered the execution of his own cousin, Ricardo de la Puente Bahamonde, with whom he had once had many arguments about politics and the army's place in society. Although in this case Franco's decision may have been difficult, in the end he chose to value consistent, cold, hard justice over family ties or sentiments of mercy. Within months of the war's outbreak, other military officers and generals also fell victim to rebel firing squads, including the man who had helped Franco run the *Academia General Militar*, Col. Miguel Campíns Aura. Campíns, who reportedly died clutching a crucifix, thus joined other officers and at least six generals who paid with their lives for failing to join the rebellion.[6]

This uncompromising attitude toward supporters of the Republic extended into the civilian world as well. One month into the war, Mola himself proclaimed that the Nationalists were waging "a war without concessions. If I see my own father among the enemy's ranks, I'll kill him."[7] And the Nationalists had espoused this kind of rhetoric from the beginning. Spain may have had a long tradition of relatively peaceful and bloodless military coups, including Gen. Miguel Primo de Rivera's seizure of power a little more than a decade earlier, but this time extreme and merciless attitudes prevailed.

Yet the Republicans and their sympathizers were not the only victims of military executions and mass terror. In the areas in which they retained control, more than 900 military officers were imprisoned or executed as real or apparent enemies of the Republic. Outside the officer corps, supporters of the Republic also purged the more conservative elements of Spanish society in unprecedented numbers, slaughtering about 7,000 priests and other church figures in one of the worst clerical massacres in modern history.[8] In addition, Republican supporters killed tens of thousands of landowners, businessmen, and other more conservative members of society during the course of the war, often without giving them the benefit of any sort of trial.

This violence was rarely organized above the local level, and national Republican leaders vigorously and publicly condemned it. But before the civil war prominent leftist leaders had joined their rightist counterparts in employing ample violent and extremist rhetoric, thereby fueling the already intense climate of uncompromising hatred. In a sense, then, these leaders had also helped create the conditions for the slaughter that took place in Republican areas after the war broke out.

But the question of blame clearly meant little to the victims of Republican terror or the many more who lived in fear that it would soon reach them. Ironically, the attempted overthrow of the Republic that many of them supported had unleashed their worst nightmare: "Red" terror and revolution now struck fear in their hearts, and not without reason.

Nevertheless, it cannot be said that the Republican terror alone explains the brutal Nationalist purgings of suspected opponents in occupied territories. The repression by Franco's forces was not simply a reaction to the Republican terror; instead, it was a logical, conscious component of Franco's way of war. On the most basic level, his methods freed him from the fear of insurgencies behind enemy lines. As we have seen in Morocco, enemy soldiers and civilians alike suffered harsh punishments aimed at discouraging further resistance, and many officers came to view such measures as a normal part of war. Tellingly, a 1938 operational manual for rebel division commanders called for the purging of political opponents in conquered villages—a practice it termed "radical cleansing"—in the same dry, logical manner in which it instructed readers on the more technical aspects of military operations, from the removal of mines to the tactical employment of artillery and armored cars. Such doctrine and language may have reflected in part the dehumanizing effects of the Moroccan war and the hatred of some conservative officers like Franco for the "godless Marxists" they were now fighting. Widespread violence against civilians also demonstrated that the Spanish Civil War was, sadly enough, not a unique case in modern history: such terror has been a common component in many civil wars, including those in twentieth-century Russia, Yugoslavia, Greece, and Finland.[9]

Some Spanish Insurgents showed sympathy for their military and political opponents, viewing them as unfortunate but necessary victims of the war. The Nationalist Lt. Rafael González Toro was especially struck by "the sad women dressed in mourning, exemplifying the wave of grief invading Spain," whom he encountered as he moved into recently conquered areas. He paradoxically described his work as part of a military "cleansing column" as "sad" but mitigated by "the belief in the necessity of our mission and the noble graciousness with which we are received all over."[10]

The Nationalists and their allies also killed civilians from the air. The most famous bombing of Republican territory occurred at the hands of German and Italian pilots at Guernica in the Basque Country on 26 April 1937 and inspired Pablo Picasso to paint his famous artistic protest against the war. In Madrid, Barcelona, and elsewhere civilians also lost their lives during the civil war in air raids, which contributed even further to the already horrible and often deadly trauma of the war for Spanish society.

It should not be forgotten, though, that Franco and his generals were hardly the only military leaders to view the bombing of cities and crucial industrial areas as legitimate means of pursuing war. The Republicans themselves sometimes bombed enemy population centers, conducting highly destructive retaliatory raids on Salamanca and Sevilla that, according to an American diplomat at the time, triggered widespread panic and the flight of thousands of civilians. And in a more general context, after World War I, many air force leaders had come to see civilians as legitimate targets, often advocating far more massive and deadly attacks than those that actually took place on Spanish soil. In the 1920s, for instance, U.S. Chief of Air Staff Billy Mitchell suggested the burning of Japanese cities should war with Japan break out, even though on other occasions he had written that civilians were not legitimate targets for air attacks. He also considered the possibility of using poison gas to contaminate water supplies and thereby impel the evacuation of cities.[11]

In other words, what became known as "strategic bombing" during World War II was not a novel idea—at least not in the world of western military thought. Hence, it was not surprising that Franco and his allies sometimes bombed cities, although they never went as far as to seek strategic victory through air attacks alone. When the war had first broken out, the U.S. military attaché in Madrid expected the air war to escalate quickly to levels not yet seen in Europe, considering it noteworthy when chemical weapons were *not* used.

As became clear during World War II, however, civilians can be more resilient in the face of air attacks than the proponents of strategic bombing predicted. As another foreign military observer wrote in January, "One of the remarkable features of the war so far has been the amount of punishment the inhabitants of Madrid have taken from bombardment." Thus, he continued, the expectations of military theorists that "continual bombardment of a civil population would completely disorganize the community life" had clearly proved wrong. Ineffective and not employed as a strategic weapon on its own, most of the Nationalist bombing served tactical aims in conjunction with ground campaigns, such as the initial Nationalist attempts to take Madrid.[12]

In a more specific observation, the American attaché's office also expressed surprise when, after taking Badajoz, Franco's forces took another detour in the fall of 1936 on their way from southern Spain to Madrid. This time the medieval city of Toledo was the objective. In the view of the attaché, Franco's failure to take the capital when he apparently could have was "a fatal mistake."[13] By early September the legionnaires and *Regulares* under the command of Yagüe had reached striking distance of Madrid, having pushed the disorganized, reorganized Republican army to the point where it had to take a stand. But Franco decided to make a stop first in Toledo. There some 2,000 Nationalist troops and sympathizers were besieged in its famous fortress, the Alcázar, which housed the Infantry Academy where Franco had begun his military career.

According to church documents, during the first part of the war more than 700 people lost their lives to Republican violence in Toledo, a city of only about 25,000 inhabitants. Among the murdered were more than forty priests. Not surprisingly, the

Civil Guardsmen, members of the Falange (the Spanish Fascist Party that supported Franco), officers, cadets, and other conservatives who had taken refuge in the Alcázar feared the worst if the fortress fell to the Republicans. In the end, though, Loyalists also died in great numbers in Toledo. As was often the case, much blood was shed when the *Regulares* and the Legion units fought their way into the town. Subsequently, an American journalist even claimed that he had seen the beheaded corpses of Republican militiamen, a sight that would not have been too surprising to anyone familiar with the Army of Africa. On 28 September, the commander of the operation, Gen. José Enrique Varela, entered the Alcázar which much fanfare.[14]

When in October the Nationalists again focused their endeavors on Madrid, they faced more formidable resistance than earlier. Soviet tanks, planes, pilots, and other assistance arrived in the capital, and the continued organization and growth of the Republican forces soon made them a more than sufficient match for the attacking Nationalists. Early November brought the arrival of the Communist-organized International Brigades, consisting of foreigners who volunteered to join the fight against Franco. Although the Nationalists received aid of their own from Germany and Italy, by now Madrid was better defended than before.[15]

The Nationalists first tried to break through the defensive forces around the Mazanares River to the west of Madrid with frontal attacks. Before attempting to cross the river, the Nationalist general staff ordered Junker planes to bomb the western part of the city. Although some optimists in the rebel camp expected immediate surrender to result, when the Nationalist infantry attacked it failed to gain much ground. The Nationalists then tried to outflank the northern defensive line three times, the last time in early January. Each of these attempts ended in failure. But their character forshadowed on a smaller scale how Franco's forces at times prosecuted the war with what has been described as the classic military "indirect approach."[16] In other words, Franco was in fact capable of favoring maneuver over direct assaults and attritional campaigns, regardless of what some of his critics have written. On the other hand, however, the argument that the indirect approach consistently and consciously defined his strategy throughout the war is not valid.

Not surprisingly, even during the war Franco's strategy had its critics. A French military report, written by someone who—like the American attaché—was generally more sympathetic to the Insurgents than to the Republicans, questioned Franco's decision to focus on Madrid in the first place. It argued that Franco should have cut off Republican supply routes from Valencia instead of concentrating on the central theater. According to the report, Franco's desire to relieve the besieged Alcázar in Toledo explained his focus on the Madrid area. In the French observer's words, "a local episode caused him to abandon good strategy for a plan based on sentiment." The report continued:

> The history of the first resistance of Madrid is replete with lost opportunities on the part of the nationalist commanders. Timidity, lack of vision . . . prevailed together with internal difficulties and the lack of reserves. As the weeks go by, one is astonished that General Franco has neither reestablished direct communication with old Castille by surrounding the small groups of militia entrenched in the Sierra, nor has he cut the important supply artery—the Valencia-Madrid road.[17]

From a purely military perspective such criticism made some sense, but it overlooked political considerations in a way Franco never would.

Two weeks after the French attaché made his observations, the Nationalists did in fact make a move that—if successful—would have eventually cut the supply route between Madrid and Valencia. The maneuver consisted of attacking eastward across the Jarama River south of the city in an attempt to outflank the Republicans' southern defensive line. On 6 February more than 18,000 Nationalist troops launched the attack, but after a week the momentum began to shift in favor of the Republicans. With the help of well-motivated International Brigade troops, the Republicans brought the Nationalists to a halt by the end of the month, although they also exhausted their own resources.

The Battle of Jarama was the bloodiest thus far of the war, with total casualty estimates ranging from 6,000 to 20,000. It involved German, Italian, Soviet, and Spanish planes, American mercenary pilots, Soviet and German tanks, and ample antiaircraft and artillery fire. The Nationalist side even included a brigade of Irish recruited by the radical rightist Eoin O'Duffy, although it saw little action. The battle also saw a higher level of air-ground coordination than before, and in more technically demanding operations, even the Republicans showed notable improvement. With relatively few well-qualified men, the Loyalist artillery corps demonstrated that it had already learned much during the fighting around Madrid. Casualties in the Republican infantry, however, continued to be high, in no small part because learning through experience was a far deadlier process in this corps than it was for the artillery. The Nationalist infantry may also have suffered from its lack of previous experience; according to O'Duffy's Irish volunteers, the Spaniards had not dug their trenches properly because they had not learned how to do so in World War I.[18]

At this point Franco finally gave into the pressure of his Italian allies, who had proved an increasing bother to Franco with their criticism of his methods and their insistence that they play a more prominent role in the conflict. In early March he allowed the Italians to launch an attack toward Guadalajara, a town northeast of Madrid. The attack failed in its goal of cutting off Madrid from the east, and the Italian defeat gave the Republicans a much needed, well-publicized psychological victory. For Franco, however, this apparent setback was not necessarily a cause of major concern.

In fact, Franco may even have helped facilitate the Italian defeat by withholding Spanish reinforcements; at any rate, he was certainly pleased with the attack's function as a distraction from Nationalist operations in the south. It is doubtful that he wished for a major defeat of any Nationalist forces—whether Spanish,

Italian, or otherwise—but on the other hand, a great victory by the Italians would have forced him to heed outside advice more readily. Indeed, he had only reluctantly allowed the Italians a greater voice in Nationalist planning after the humiliation of the Jarama attack. Given his stubborn nature and his desire to hold complete control of military, as well as political, actions within the rebel camp, Franco probably regarded an unexpectedly hard struggle for the Italians at Guadalajara as a small price to pay to maintain his power and more long-term aims. From this point on the Italians had less say in the leadership of Nationalist military operations, even though their influence on the internal political scene in Francoist Spain remained strong. In the meantime, moreover, Italian forces had successfully aided rebel forces in southern Spain, and the Nationalists had taken control of Málaga on 8 February.

After the Battle of Guadalajara, the Nationalist center of gravity shifted from the Madrid front to the northern theater, and any thoughts of a quick decision appeared to be entirely absent from Franco's mind. Under the initial direction of Mola, the Nationalists eventually achieved victory in the northern theater, with the port city of Bilbao falling on 19 June and the rest of the Vizcaya region shortly thereafter. It took several more months for the Nationalists to conquer the Republican areas in Asturias to the west, which they finally gained full control of in October.

By deciding to shift his main point of focus to the north, possibly at the urging of one or more of his generals, Franco had achieved Nationalist superiority in overall resources. But the rather slow campaign, which included the infamous bombing of Guernica, also saw Mola's death when his plane crashed into a mountain on 3 June en route to a meeting with Franco in Salamanca. The accident so frightened Franco, whose side had already lost General Sanjurjo to a plane crash early in the war, that he avoided flying for the rest of his life.

Hoping to divert the Nationalists from their focus on the northern campaign, more than 60,000 Republican troops launched a surprise offensive near the town of Brunete, north-west of Madrid, in early July. They initially broke through the Nationalist line but then hesitated to continue their thrust, in part due to difficulties with communications and logistics. Franco sent in reinforcements from the north and elsewhere, which managed to push the front line back nearly to its original position. According to the subsequent comments of leading Republican commanders, the Nationalists might well have taken Madrid had they continued their drive, given the exhaustion and low morale of the Republican forces. Not surprisingly, though, Franco chose not to pursue a decisive battle.

In what was becoming a pattern, Franco faced another Republican surprise attack in late August that was meant to serve as a strategic diversion, this time on the Aragon front in the northeast. The Republican forces, totaling more than 80,000 troops, succeeded in taking the town of Belchite after a two-week siege, but the much more important city of Zaragoza remained in Nationalist hands. In mid-December the Republicans struck again on the Aragon front in the area around Teruel, enduring freezing temperatures, snow, and ample frostbite without adequate clothing or boots.[19]

Predictably enough, Franco responded by bringing in reinforcements. The Nationalists began their successful counterattack on Christmas Day, reoccupying the city on 22 February 1938, after a flank offensive on Alfambra. During the Battle of Teruel Franco's stubbornness in the face of German and Italian exhortations surfaced again. His foreign advisors implored him to draw back and concede the territory, which held little real value anyway. But Franco characteristically refused to let the Republicans hold on to any territory that they gained from the Nationalists. Instead his infantry gradually retook the territory, only advancing after what an American attaché called "great masses of artillery and aviation" first weakened the Republican resistance. According to the attaché, the Nationalists thereby debilitated the enemy by attrition and could then advance with relatively few losses of their own.[20]

Meanwhile, the Nationalists continued their gradual but steady gains in the East, reaching the Mediterranean coast at Viñaroz, between Valencia and Barcelona, on 15 April. The Republican zone was now cut in two in the East. Once again, Franco made a military decision of extreme caution, provoking yet more criticism. Instead of moving northeast through Catalonia and seizing Spain's second-largest city, Barcelona, he chose to move southwest toward Valencia. As American diplomatic reports indicate, Barcelona was suffering under enemy bombs, including those that brought down entire buildings by exploding only after penetrating deeply into the structure. With the circumstances becoming dire and shortages an ever growing problem, city authorities felt the need to take increasingly drastic measures against defeatism, hoarding, profiteering, and even treason. But Franco failed to move against the faltering city.

His surprising decision stemmed in part from the international climate, which he feared might sour in reaction to the occupation of the French border by German- and Italian-supported Nationalist troops. An outflanking attack against his forces by the French even seemed possible. Indeed, before the Western powers failed to stand up to Hitler at September's Munich conference, it was unclear how far the Western democracies would go with their policy of appeasement. Hitler himself was unsure whether other countries would act against him. Franco knew, moreover, of the plans that France's military had drawn up for a possible war with Spain, and he did not want to give the French an excuse to consider implementing them. Because of such worries, his diplomats repeatedly sought to assure their British and French colleagues of Spanish neutrality in any European conflict that might break out. In this context, his decision not to direct his forces toward northern Catalonia in a major attack makes more sense.[21]

In July the Republicans launched their final major offensive of the war, a massive surprise attack of three army corps across the Ebro River. After their engineers constructed pontoon bridges during the night of 24–25 July, the Republicans attacked. Franco's reaction was not unexpected; he brought in reinforcements and after initially suffering significant losses, slowly retook the ground his forces had initially lost.

The Battle of the Ebro exemplified the operational superiority of the Nationalists in many ways. Their tactics during the first part of the counterattack included directing their firepower at insufficiently fortified Republican positions. They then attacked the positions under close air support, machine-gunning the fleeing enemy forces. Throughout the counteroffensive, they benefited from careful, methodical preparations of their air force and artillery. As a result, a barrier of artillery fire protected the infantry, which advanced behind a curtain of smoke and fire. The Nationalist planes, moreover, used chain bombing techniques with considerable efficacy.

In contrast, Republican air power failed to appear when most needed. And even though the Republican artillery corps had improved since the beginning of the war, it still lacked the kind of experienced talent that its Nationalist counterpart enjoyed. In fact, by September 1938 only 14 percent of the Republic's veteran artillerymen remained on the official officer list. For this reason, the Republicans could not employ their big guns in the sophisticated fashion of their enemies. Admittedly, the performance of Franco's forces had its bad moments as well. At times, they suffered greatly during the battle, especially during the initial Republican onslaught. But overall the Nationalists executed their operations more skillfully than did their opponents, who— thanks in part to command and logistic weaknesses—failed once again to exploit their early success.[22]

In spite of their most valiant efforts, then, the Republicans again lost on the battlefield. But victories in battle had long ceased to mean much from the perspective of grand strategy anyway. As Franco and many others were well aware, the final result of the war had long become a foregone conclusion, especially after the British and other Western powers failed to stand up to Hitler in Munich.

During the last part of the war, Franco received overtures from Republican representatives to negotiate an end to the

The Battle of the Ebro, 1938

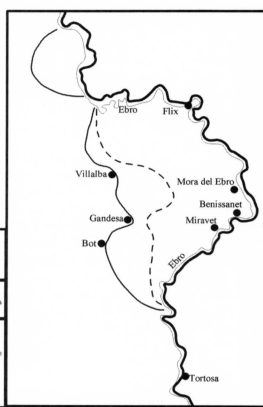

Don P. Green, Jr.
USM- Dept. of
Geography

Scale

5   0   5   10 Miles

Inset

Spain

Eastern Ebro River

Ebro
Flix
Villalba
Mora del Ebro
Benissanet
Gandesa
Miravet
Bot
Ebro
Tortosa

Legend

∿ River

- - - Front Lines on
Sept. 30, 1938

● Towns

∿ Furthest Advance
by Republicans

∿ Front Lines on
July 23, 1938

conflict, but he categorically rejected any concessions or negotiations. As he had demonstrated with the Nationalist repression in occupied territories throughout the war, Franco meant to destroy all possible Republican resistance. His policy of destruction served to consolidate his personal position of power in the new Spain that he created.

On 26 January 1939 the Nationalists took Barcelona, and they reached the French border on 5 February. By the end of February, Britain and France both had recognized Franco's government officially, and on 28 March his troops entered Madrid. The last Republican units in Spain surrendered on 1 April, and that day Franco announced the end of the civil war.

Even before the civil war ended, observers had begun to pass judgment on Franco's military leadership. Of course, inside Franco's Spain no one publicly expressed anything but praise. Often discounting the vital aid provided by Nazi Germany and Fascist Italy, the dictatorship's supporters lauded the *caudillo* in glowing terms for his allegedly masterful direction of the Nationalist war efforts. The Republican exiles and their sympathizers, on the other hand, often stressed the German and Italian aid, glossing over the Soviet assistance they themselves had received, their own military shortcomings, and the successes of Franco's command in general.

Today, with the benefit of hindsight, how should we assess Franco's military thought? He undoubtedly profited—at times decisively—from the support of his foreign fascist allies and the failings and weaknesses of his enemies. Moreover, the international climate of appeasement and the related neutral stances of democratic powers, including France, Great Britain, and the United States, worked to his advantage.

Franco also benefited from a unified political front that the Republican side never came close to matching. By October 1936 his fellow generals made him supreme leader and commander of Nationalist Spain, and he eliminated most possible political rivals within the rebel camp. Early in the war Republican sympathizers killed José Antonio Primo de Rivera, the leader of the Spanish Fascist Party, the Falange. The death of José Antonio, who was the son of the late dictator of the 1920s, gave the Franco government the opportunity to transform the Falange's original, more radical and revolutionary, program into one that better suited its interests. Francoist propagandists could then use the Falange as a source of ideological support for a war that was proving to be more difficult than they had initially expected. In the so-called unification decree of 19 April 1937, Franco merged the Falange with another extreme right-wing group, the Carlists, and some smaller conservative parties. The strongly Catholic, monarchist, and tradition-obsessed Carlists rejected the more radical aspects of the original Falangist doctrine, but Franco forced the two groups together into one political organization regardless. In this way, he effectively created a fascist-style, one-party state. In addition, the church provided him with key support throughout the war.

Yet these undeniably crucial ingredients in his victory in the civil war should not obscure assessments of his military leadership itself. Ironically, even though Franco's primary identity was that of a soldier, his political skills often outshone his military thinking during the civil war. But the two were not unrelated, and what did not make sense in purely military terms sometimes appeared more logical in the greater context of Franco's desire to secure absolute power for himself. His wartime diplomacy also proved effective, yielding important benefits to his side that his enemies could not equal. Moreover, his military thought evolved somewhat over time, and while he was not without his faults on the battlefield, the skills he did enjoy as a a military commander and thinker proved increasingly propitious during the course of the conflict. Indeed, he became the first military leader in Spain since 1814 to maneuver corps and field armies.

During the first days after the rebels took up arms, Franco and Mola's strategy consisted of little more than reaching Madrid and declaring victory. The movement of Franco's army from the south had little coordination with Mola's in the north, and Franco thus failed to send extra troops to the northern front when they might have proved decisive. In general, he and Mola seemed to have had little appreciation for the need to coordinate diverse tactical actions systematically in order to achieve a single strategic goal; in other words, they had little appreciation for the operational level of war. As we have seen, the operational level of war falls between and links together tactics and strategy, and encompasses what Clausewitz called "grand tactics" and what others prefer to situate within the realm of strategy. When the operational-level planning is ideal, the end result of all tactical actions will exceed the sum of their parts.[23]

At the onset of the war, the Nationalist leadership displayed scant operational awareness, in part because they had the typical disdain of professional soldiers for amateur militia forces. As critics have rightly noted, Franco's unimaginative, plodding strategy during the first part of the war may well have cost the Nationalists a rapid victory. Instead of attempting to seize Madrid before the Republicans could organize themselves sufficiently, he ambled northward at a very gradual pace, sending troops as far west as the Portuguese border to secure his flank, sowing terror along the way, and then taking a detour at Toledo.

Franco clearly had no interest in employing anything resembling the tactics of what came to be known as *Blitzkrieg*, or lightning war, after the Germans' rapid defeats of Poland and France during World War II. In any case, he lacked the armored vehicles those kind of attacks require. But even on a more general level, the idea of rapid military advances barely figured in his strategic thought.

In addition to the painfully slow march toward Madrid, the Nationalists moved at a protracted pace in their year-long endeavors beginning in October 1936 to close the pocket of Republican resistance in the northern theater, although here mountainous terrain made quicker movement more difficult. In both cases, the argument that Franco simply wanted to annihilate all resistance and secure complete control before moving onward is only part of the story; his more fundamental inability to consider the methods that a *Blitzkrieg*-style campaign would have entailed made talk of a possible lightning victory irrelevant in the first place.[24]

Later in the war, though, Franco's cautious approach made more sense, and his coordination of actions in different theaters improved over that in the earlier phases of the war. Critics, then and now, have argued that Franco missed opportunities throughout the war for decisive attacks akin to the German invasion and rapid defeat of the Netherlands, Belgium, and France in 1940. According to these critics, Franco should have waged *Blitzkrieg*, and in so doing, he could have affected a Napoleonic-style decisive battle. But the criticism of Franco for not waging *Blitzkrieg*—a concept never precisely defined—overlooks some fundamental points.

The rapid German victory over France in 1940 that critics believe Franco should have anticipated was not an inevitability. In fact, it surprised virtually everyone. Hitler's own generals worried that they would become bogged down quickly, turning the battle into a massive, long, and bloody fight. Until its defeat by the Germans, the French army was considered the best in Europe. In today's computer simulations of the battle, the Germans lose. Only a combination of luck, excellent tactical skills, and French failings made Germany's victory in so little time possible.[25]

On a more general level, moreover, even if plans for bold and dramatic maneuvers have more appeal than slow and bloody attrition, when they fail the result can be disastrous. World War I began on the western front with a daring and ambitious sweep through Belgium, but when this strategy failed to achieve rapid victory, years of attrition followed. In World War II the so-called *Blitzkrieg* approach fell short against the Soviet Union. The Germans achieved unprecedented tactical victories, killing hundreds of thousands of enemy troops during the first part of the campaign, but there was no decisive battle. Instead, sound operational-level planning and execution, referred to by the Soviets as "operational art," combined with advantages of space, manpower, material, and unforseen developments on other fronts to bring victory to the Soviet Union.

In terms of strategic and operational thinking, World War II's eastern front and the Spanish Civil War had more in common than it appears at first glance. Admittedly, Soviet writings on operational art generally focused on very large-scale warfare that far exceeded the scope of the Spanish Civil War, and American writings on the operational level of war often treat its quantitative dimension as integral to its definition. The Soviets classified "fronts," or armies, as "operational," and the Spanish Civil War clearly did not see such massive units as would characterize the eastern front in World War II. But the tendency among some military writers today to think in such a quantitative fashion may obscure the conceptual heart of the term, not unlike the way the adjective "strategic" has come to refer to long-range missiles even when their purpose is actually tactical.

In fact, it was the history of conflicts such as the Franco-Prussian War, the Russo-Japanese War, and World War I that the Soviets initially drew upon when developing their concept of the operational level, even if they first applied it on a massive scale in World War II. Furthermore, a crucial element in the development of Soviet operational thinking was the repudiation of the idea of the decisive battle.[26] By at least 1937, Franco himself may have better understood the growing irrelevance of this idea than many of his critics at the time and some historians even today.

During World War II the Soviets themselves deemed the lessons of the Spanish Civil War relevant to their own vastly larger armed forces. In fact, leading Soviet military thinkers carefully studied the Spanish conflict, considering it—as one historian of Soviet doctrine writes—"a valid picture of a future large-scale war." Their belief that the civil war exemplified modern war in general and thus merited close analysis only became stronger as the fighting in Spain continued. While making allowances for differences between the situation in Spain and what they thought Soviet forces might face in the future, they drew lessons about infantry-armor cooperation, command and communication, and

Cadets from the Infantry Academy in Toledo, where Franco studied from 1907 to 1910. Franco and his classmates at the academy often practiced tactics more appropriate for regular warfare than the counterinsurgency campaigns they would wage in Morocco after graduation. *Author's Collection*

Infantry Academy cadets practice setting up camp. Franco's performance as a cadet was unspectacular, revealing few if any signs of the heights to which he would one day rise as an officer. *Author's Collection*

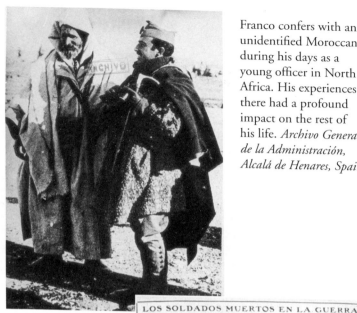

Franco confers with an unidentified Moroccan during his days as a young officer in North Africa. His experiences there had a profound impact on the rest of his life. *Archivo General de la Administración, Alcalá de Henares, Spain*

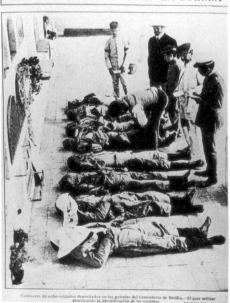

LOS SOLDADOS MUERTOS EN LA GUERRA

The bodies of several Spanish soldiers killed in the Moroccan war are examined and identified by a military investigator. Nearly 1,000 Spanish officers and 16,000 of their soldiers met their deaths in North Africa while Franco was serving there. *Archivo General de la Administración, Alcalá de Henares, Spain*

Spanish troops disembark at Al Hoceima Bay, Morocco, after establishing a beachhead. Franco later wrote a dramatic, self-serving account of how he led his men to shore during the first wave of the attack. *Archivo General de la Administración, Alcalá de Henares, Spain*

An aerial photo of a Spanish naval landing in Morocco. Franco took part in the 1925 amphibious operation at Al Hoceima Bay, which employed the same landing craft that the British had used at Gallipoli, albeit with notably more success. Air, naval, and land forces from Spain and France along with native Moroccan troops participated in the operation and eventual defeat of Moroccan leader Abd al-Karim. *Archivo General de la Administración, Alcalá de Henares, Spain*

El general Arizón sujetando una bandera para envolver con ella los restos de un oficial encontrados en el barranco del Lobo

General Arizón observes the draping of a Spanish flag over the remains of an officer found in the Wolf Ravine in Morocco. In the summer of 1909 Moroccan insurgents ambushed Spanish forces in the ravine, resulting in nearly 1,000 Spanish casualties, including around 180 deaths. *Archivo General de la Administración, Alcalá de Henares, Spain*

A military encampment in Morocco. In addition to using its own regular army troops, Spain enlisted Moroccans in its endeavors to wipe out native resistance to colonial rule. *Archivo General de la Administración, Alcalá de Henares, Spain*

The Spanish military post at Ben Karrich, Morocco. Although Spaniards employed motorized vehicles and even a few tanks during the Moroccan campaigns, they relied on animals for the bulk of their transportation needs. *Author's Collection*

An artillery unit on its way to Spanish positions at Sidi Ahmet al-Hach, Morocco. Unlike many of his fellow infantrymen, Franco praised the artillery corps and stressed its importance to military operations in general. *Archivo General de la Administración, Alcalá de Henares, Spain*

Nationalists march triumphantly out of the Alcázar in Toledo after its liberation by Franco's forces in late September 1936. The Alcázar was home to the Infantry Academy where Franco began his military life as a fourteen-year-old cadet. During the Spanish Civil War, Franco's decision to lift the siege of the Alcázar in late 1936 instead of moving directly toward Madrid provoked much criticism, but it also gained him a significant public relations victory. *Archivo General de la Administración, Alcalá de Henares, Spain*

Along with Nazi Germany, Mussolini's Fascist Italy provided Franco with vital support during the Spanish Civil War. Here Spanish civilians watch from balconies as Italian forces pass by.
Archivo General de la Administración, Alcalá de Henares, Spain

Franco surveys the situation during the Battle of the Ebro, 1938. After being thrown back by a massive surprise attack across the Ebro River, the Nationalists recovered and pushed the Republicans back. *Archivo General de la Administración, Alcalá de Henares, Spain*

Nationalist troops attack during their counteroffensive in the Battle of the Ebro, 1938.
Archivo General de la Administración, Alcalá de Henares, Spain

Franco, his wife Carmen, and Prince Juan Carlos during the latter part of the dictatorship. As Franco had decided, Juan Carlos assumed the title of King of Spain after the caudillo's death. In opposition to his wishes, however, the new king then promoted Spain's transition to democracy. *Archivo General de la Administración, Alcalá de Henares, Spain*

Franco with unidentified Arab leaders. After World War II the Franco dictatorship attempted to foster what it claimed was a "special relationship" with the Arab world. *Archivo General de la Administración, Alcalá de Henares, Spain*

Franco and his wife Carmen walking out of a church. The church and the military, along with the Spanish Fascist Party, the Falange, provided Franco with crucial support from the outbreak of the civil war in 1936 until his death in 1975. *Archivo General de la Administración, Alcalá de Henares, Spain*

An elderly Franco at a religious procession, accompanied by Prince Juan Carlos to his right. Franco's health worsened notably during the last years of his life, especially after the assassination of his most intimate and faithful collaborator, Adm. Luis Carrero Blanco, by the Basque terrorist group ETA in 1973. *Archivo General de la Administración, Alcalá de Henares, Spain*

More fundamentally, the German way of war that critics claim Franco should have anticipated was a failure overall, regardless of what happened in 1940. The undeniable tactical skills and successes of the twentieth-century German military often obscure a greater truth: in wars the Germans always met defeat. Tactical victories, however great, mean little if they fail to produce strategic victory, as World War II made clear. The German tactics that earn so much praise did not exist in a vacuum; they were only one component—albeit a very important one—of the German way of war as a whole. The strategic and operational-level thinking that ultimately failed the German army was also crucial.

In some ways the Spanish Civil War may not have resembled the modern industrial warfare of World War II as much as the often static western front of World War I. But, as the American Civil War had already suggested and both world wars confirmed, the decisive battle was losing its relevance, at least in wars in which no side enjoyed a huge material advantage. Modern industry and technology, with the accompanying increase in defensive firepower, had made decisive attacks and maneuvers less effective. During the Moroccan war, Franco himself had learned to discourage thoughts of definitive victories, advocating instead the use of the same elements the Soviets used on a much greater scale to defeat Germany in World War II: time, hunger, exhaustion, and attrition in general. Moreover, Franco's gradual approach favored the Nationalists over their Republican opponents, who—like the German army on the eastern front—proved incapable of meeting the basic needs of their troops.[28]

Of course, the comparison between the military thought of Franco and Stalin's generals should not be pushed too far. Franco lacked the foresight and intellectual depth of Soviet military thinkers like Tukhachevskii, Svechin, and many of their colleagues. Moreover, Franco's refusal to concede tactical ground for strategic benefit stood in direct opposition to what the Soviets learned to do with great effectiveness in World War II.

Franco's approach to the Spanish Civil War did not result from the conscious development of sophisticated and pathbreaking doctrine, as had happened in the Soviet Union.

But Franco had the good fortune to have developed his military thought in Morocco, where final victory had entailed careful, methodical advances and relatively well-planned and coordinated joint force and combined operations, such as that at Al Hoceima Bay. He could also better afford the casualties that his stubborn refusals to give up territory yielded. Even though neither the planning nor the execution of the Moroccan campaigns represented the complete realization of operational art, they did happen to include some of its key ingredients, albeit on a much smaller scale. Nationalist war-fighting doctrine repeatedly emphasized and explained in detail cooperation within and between different arms, including artillery, infantry, cavalry, air force, and engineers, as the Francoist wartime manual for division commanders attested.[29]

The Republicans, on the other hand, executed even well-planned operations with notably less skill than did the Nationalists, as the Battle of the Ebro demonstrated. The initial gains of Republican tanks on the battlefield usually foundered without the support they needed from other units, and their air force often failed to appear at all when most needed. Moreover, coordination between tanks and the artillery was even worse than that between the infantry and armored units.[30]

What accounts for the difference in operational proficiency? It may well have stemmed largely from the far greater number of experienced professional officers, often with *africanista* backgrounds, who offered their talents to Franco's side. Although most generals remained loyal to the Republic or avoided taking any action at all when the war first broke out, overall a very small portion of the officer corps chose to serve the Republican armed forces.[31] Franco thus had at his disposal an officer corps with far more experience and technical expertise. Indeed, some of the support staff Franco relied heavily upon in the war—such as the future tutor to King Juan Carlos, Gen. Carlos Martinez de Campos of the artillery corps—were intelligent, learned, and perhaps most importantly, highly experienced on the battlefield.

The Republicans could also boast of some very bright military leaders, such as Gen. Vicente Rojo, whose writings reveal far more intellectual ability than those of Franco. But Rojo's excellent staff work was not matched by extensive practical experiences in Morocco of the kind Franco had behind him. Moreover, Rojo could not draw upon as many experienced, professional officers for planning and executing military operations. He also had to deal with troublesome Soviet advisors and their partial control of much of the Republic's armored and air forces.

Unlike Rojo, Franco had acquired relatively little textbook knowledge and few sophisticated ideas as a cadet and in staff college. He had little more than his practical experiences from which to develop his military thought. But fortuitously for him, these experiences proved especially apt in the civil war: they served to reinforce his and his officers' awareness of the importance of combined-arms coordination and the overall strategic design that each tactical action had to serve, or in today's terms, their operational-level planning.

Chapter 6

Dictatorship to Death: 1939–75

Franco's victory in the Spanish Civil War brought his days as a military commander to an end. From 1939 on, he led not on the battlefield, but at the helm of Spain's national government. As the *caudillo*, or supreme leader, he had final say over economic, social, diplomatic, political, and even cultural affairs in Spain. But throughout his decades-long dictatorship he also relied on several institutions for vital support: the military, the church, and the Falange. Of these three, the military was the most important. The armed forces did not make policies during the dictatorship, but they guaranteed that the caudillo's policies were carried out.

Franco's identity as a very conservative, combat-hardened infantry officer remained as strong as ever, shaping the character and overall development of the country for decades to come. Even though the rebel military forces had finally brought the Second Republic to a definitive end, in many ways Franco kept Spain on a war footing throughout World War II and thereafter. Instead of attempting to heal the country through reconciliation, the caudillo implemented policies based on the same principles of punishment and purification that had shaped his views throughout the civil war. Like his ultra-conservative interpretation of Christianity, his treatment of past and present dissenters reflected an unwavering belief in the righteousness of his cause and in using force and discipline to achieve national regeneration.

During the civil war more than 100,000 people were executed behind the lines by either Nationalist or Republican gunmen. When combined with the even greater number of Spanish combat fatalities during the war, the end effect was a considerable death toll for both sides. But the cruelty did not end when the guns fell silent. Franco, whose side lost even more lives to wartime repression than did the Loyalists, showed little mercy for the defeated.

After the war, at least thirty-four camps and dozens of prisons all over Spain held men and women deemed enemies of Franco's Spain. In May 1940 these facilities still held some 240,000 prisoners, nearly 8,000 of whom had received the death sentence. Others still awaited their sentencing. All together at least 28,000 Spaniards were shot under the orders of the Franco government after the war.

Before the war came to an end, Franco had already demonstrated a personal interest in pursuing severe punitive measures against his enemies. By the late winter of 1937, he was personally reviewing the death sentences that military courts meted out for political crimes, occasionally going as far as to order that the condemned be strangled to death by a metal collar (*garrote*). He also ordered the press to cover some of these executions.

While reviewing these sentences, Franco acted in his capacity as commander in chief of the armed forces and not as the political head of Nationalist Spain. As always, his military identity predominated. Martial law remained in effect until April 1948, and even thereafter all serious political offenses were tried by court martial. When Franco's brother-in-law and close advisor, Ramón Serrano Súñer, argued that he needed to act more in accordance with accepted legal standards, Franco reminded him that soldiers disliked civilian interference with "the application of their code of justice."[1]

In other matters, however, Serrano Súñer views were more in accordance with those of the caudillo. Serrano, a member of the Falange who embraced the party's radical, fascist heritage far more enthusiastically than many other Franco supporters, was a strong supporter of Nazi Germany during much of World War II, and the caudillo shared much of his enthusiasm for Hitler's military successes. Although Franco was too much of a traditional conservative to adopt the more radical aspects of Nazism, he praised Hitler's Germany in various speeches and used similar propaganda to project an image at least somewhat based on that of the Führer. And to an even greater degree, he adopted the trappings of the original Fascist dictator, Italy's Benito Mussolini.

In addition to delivering triumphant speeches at large, fascist-style rallies all over Spain, the caudillo made his presence known in portraits and murals, on the faces of stamps and coins, and in school textbooks and other publications that disseminated an image of magnificent, paternalistic power. By employing widespread censorship, requiring those who wished to advance professionally to join government-run institutions, and mandating Falangist organizations for men, women, and children, the Franco regime resembled Fascist Italy and Nazi Germany in many ways. Franco was certainly not as murderous of a leader as Hitler or Stalin, but the number of Spaniards who lost their lives or otherwise suffered under his rule was nonetheless substantial, especially during the first part of his dictatorship.

During most of World War II, moreover, Franco believed that Hitler would emerge victorious and that dictatorships faced a brighter future than did democracy. Although he never actively joined forces with the Axis powers, he provided them with some logistic support, sent workers to aid Germany's war economy, and allowed the creation of the Blue Division of Spanish volunteers (officially the *División Española de Voluntarios*) to fight alongside Hitler's forces against the Soviet Union. He also allowed German submarines to refuel in Spanish waters. In fact, if Hitler had agreed to support Franco in his colonialist ambitions in North Africa, Spain might have formally joined forces with Hitler and Mussolini in World War II. But Hitler understandably valued the support of the Vichy government in France and could never agree to cede any of its North African territory to Franco. In any case, Spain's economy and armed forces were in no condition to support the country's participation in another war.

When the Allies landed in northwest Africa in November 1942, Franco found himself in a particularly uncomfortable position. Although several members of his cabinet urged him to allow German troops to pass through Spanish territory, he sided with the majority who thought otherwise. Ordering a partial mobilization of troops that temporarily swelled the ranks of soldiers on active duty, he pursued a defensive strategy intended to make the Germans think that a move into Spain would be more trouble than it was worth. At the same time, he felt reasonably certain that he could trust Roosevelt's promise that the Allies posed no threat to Spanish territory. Indeed, he felt secure enough about his own position that he continued to praise Nazi Germany and Fascist Italy in public speeches.

By early 1943, however, as the scale of the disaster at Stalingrad became apparent, the Franco government betrayed signs that its earlier faith in an inevitable Axis victory was beginning to waver. After Mussolini was overthrown in July and Italy pulled out of the war in September, Franco made increasingly more efforts to distance himself from Fascism. Although Spain continued to supply wolfram to Germany, government policies began to change more significantly by early 1944. Franco withdrew the Blue Division from the eastern front in October 1943, and its smaller successor, the Blue Legion, from the eastern front by the next March. The Spanish press, however, continued to display marked sympathies for the Germans until the end of the war.[2]

Franco's worries during World War II went beyond Spain's position vis-à-vis the Allied and Axis powers. He also had to worry about dangers to his own position from within Spain, at times even from within the ranks of the armed forces. Some of the threats to his rule came from more radical Falangists, who felt he did not go far enough in reshaping the new, Nationalist Spain. They favored transforming the country in a radical manner, with the eventual goal of implementing a true fascist revolution. But Franco was also under pressure from the Carlists and other conservatives who favored building the new Spain upon what they believed were the ideals of monarchy and Catholic tradition. Both the monarchists and the Falangists had provided Franco with key support in the civil war, but his attempt to merge the two during the conflict had not been entirely successful, and the consequences of the incomplete fusion soon became clear.

On the one hand, Serrano Súñer and a small number of generals favored policies more in line with Falangist Fascism and, correspondingly, a closer alliance with Hitler. In their eyes, Spain needed to make a more vigorous break with its past, and not just its Republican past. They wanted more drastic social changes, and they had little interest in a regime based on centuries-old values of monarchy and the Catholic Church. As head of the Falange, Serrano Súñer promoted fascist ideals by encouraging the use of the Fascist salute and staging of large, well-choreographed rallies meant to glorify Franco and, in memoriam, the Falange's founder, José Antonio Primo de Rivera. Although Serrano Súñer, who had not joined the Falange until 1936, was resented by some of the more radical Falangists of the first hour and disliked by Hitler, he was closer to them than he was to the monarchists.

In early May 1941 many prominent Falangists, disillusioned by the failure of the regime to institute their revolutionary goals and unhappy about a recent cabinet appointment by Franco, submitted letters of resignation. The resigners included Miguel Primo de Rivera, the brother of José Antonio, and his sister Pilar, who headed the Falange's women's section. Franco's response was to go directly to the defectors, offering to incorporate more Falangists—and supporters of Nazi Germany—into his regime.

His goal was to bring them under his control by giving them positions of greater prominence while making them dependent on his good grace for their power within the regime.[3]

Yet Franco faced a much greater threat to his power from the monarchists than from the Falange. Traditional conservatives of various cuts resented his refusal to establish a monarchy after winning the civil war. They did not, however, represent a serious threat until monarchists from one of the dictatorship's key institutions, the military, took action. In September 1943, seven of Franco's twelve lieutenant generals signed a letter to the caudillo requesting that he reestablish the monarchy in Spain and dissolve the Falange, thereby moving the Spanish state away from the "foreign models" of fascism. The letter was very respectful in tone, but it nevertheless represented one of the greatest political threats that Franco ever faced. Moreover, two of the generals who did not sign the letter, Francisco Gómez-Jordana and Juan Vigón, stated that they supported its contents but had refrained from signing it because they were serving as cabinet members.

Franco's response to the crisis exemplified his ability to overcome threats to his position with skillful political maneuvering. Taking advantage of the generals' failure to demand to meet with him collectively, he endeavored to bring them back into his camp by dealing with them separately and relying on the support of the generals who had not signed the letter and other officers who remained loyal.

His response to the monarchist generals was two-fold. First, he assured them that he still intended to restore the monarchy in good time, but that it would be too risky to do so now. Second, he made a number of arguments on military and diplomatic grounds. Well aware that the recent overthrow of Mussolini and subsequent withdrawal of Italy from the war had influenced the generals' actions, he contended that Germany could still prevail, claiming the Nazi power had an arsenal of "secret weapons." In October he promoted two major generals whom he deemed to be strong supporters of his rule, thereby raising the total number of lieutenant generals on his side. And, as he did during the rest of his dictatorship, he used the specter of leftist threats to retain the support of the monarchists, who may not have regarded the Franco dictatorship as their first choice but feared they might fare even worse without it.[4]

Regardless of how well Franco managed to maintain his position of power within Spain, on the international stage, his dictatorship's longevity relied as much on luck as on political skill. As we have seen, Spain's poor condition after the civil war and Hitler's refusal to give in to Franco's unrealistic demands kept Spain out of World War II, but the caudillo nonetheless believed for a time in Germany's eventual victory and would probably have joined the Axis powers had circumstances permitted. His luck continued after the defeat of Germany and Japan, when some Allied leaders briefly considered doing away with the Franco dictatorship as part of their plan to rebuild Europe according to democratic principles.

In the years following World War II, the rise of the cold war saved Franco. A fierce opponent of communism, he appealed to government and military leaders in the United States simply because he had the potential to serve as their strategic ally. When the Korean War broke out in 1950, he attempted to win more sympathy from Western powers by offering to participate in the war on the side of the United Nations forces. Soon thereafter, Spain began to have an important place in U.S. defense planning and the North Atlantic Treaty Organisation (NATO), although western European democracies refused to let Spain join the organization as long as the country remained a dictatorship.

Assuming a more pragmatic stance, policymakers in the United States chose to overlook the more negative aspects of Franco's Spain in the interest of their anti-Soviet grand strategy. As a result, the United States helped strengthen the dictatorship by providing Spain with more than $1.5 billion worth of economic aid as part of a 1953 deal to build military bases on the peninsula. After World War II, President Truman and the U.S. Congress had denied Franco Marshall Plan funds because of the repressive nature of his government. With the 1953 agreement came the first major infusion of foreign aide since the civil war, giving a significant boost to the Spanish economy and facilitating military growth.

Although the Spanish armed forces had continued to suffer from a severe lack of funds until Franco made his pact with the United States, their organization had changed considerably since the end of the civil war. The manner in which Franco restructured the military made it clear that, once the Republican threat was extinguished, he valued the maintenance of his position as caudillo over military effectiveness. During the civil war Franco had established the Ministry of National Defense to improve coordination between the different branches of service, thereby improving the Nationalists' prosecution of the operational level of war. But after the war he cast aside the emphasis on combined arms warfare that he had once considered so important. Now, his strategy was to "divide and rule" by making the army, navy, and air force separate entities, each competing with the others for power and resources.

After the civil war the armed forces shrunk dramatically, even though the World War II compelled Franco to temper somewhat his initial military cuts. Thus in 1945 the army numbered about 365,000 troops, compared to the 900,000 serving at the end of the civil war. An excess of officers soon plagued the postwar Spanish military, reversing the Republican reforms intended to bring Spain more in line with western European standards. During the civil war Franco had curtailed promotions in an attempt to create a culture of shared military service and sacrifice, and as a result, officers and lower ranking generals commanded larger units than normal. Once he won the war, however, Franco sought to cultivate the support of the officer corps, and command responsibilities diminished while promotions increased. Because Franco made the upper levels of the officer corps far larger than necessary, it expended a significant portion of the overall military budget.

In tough economic times, military officers enjoyed a regular income, social prestige, and more access to better and affordable food than most civilians. Their salaries were not high, and it was not always easy for their families to make ends meet, but the officers nonetheless had an easier time financially than a great majority of Spaniards, and many took pride in their wartime service and their status in a regime built upon military culture and values. Former enlisted men also found their status as veterans helpful, benefiting from postwar hiring quotas. In general, Franco could count on strong, unwavering support from the bulk of the military throughout his dictatorship.

Franco divided post–civil war Spain into eight military regions on the peninsula, centered on Madrid, Barcelona, Valencia, Seville, Zaragoza, Burgos, Valladolid, and La Coruña, and two in the Spanish zone of the Moroccan protectorate. Each region was led by a lieutenant general, who received the traditional title of captain general. In addition, smaller forces manned the Balearic and Canary Islands. Still at least somewhat fearful of possible urban unrest, Franco made sure that the larger population centers—along with the North African territories—received a relatively good share of the military resources.[5]

Franco's conservative military mindset also shaped his foreign policy after World War II. Although he endeavored to reconfigure his identity from that of a Nazi supporter to that of a cold warrior and ally of Western democracies, in other ways his foreign policy aims remained markedly old-fashioned. In an era of decolonization, his regime sought to maintain its African holdings, and it repeatedly emphasized Spain's great imperial past and its status as a colonial power. Franco believed, moreover, that Spanish colonialism had little in common with its profit-driven French and British counterparts. Even after Morocco gained its independence in 1956, a very old-fashioned discourse of empire continued to characterize speeches, school textbooks, literature, and the media in Spain. Franco also appeared at public ceremonies surrounded by his colorful, traditionally-dressed Moorish Honor Guard, thereby propagating his image as an imperial leader.

The regime attempted to counter the international ostracism

it faced as a dictatorship by expanding relations with Arab countries, arguing that Spain alone had special cultural and historic ties to the Arab world. But as is often the case, rhetoric differed from reality. Despite allowing arms to be smuggled from the Spanish zone of the North African protectorate to the anti-French Moroccan freedom fighters, Franco could not win significant support from Spain's Arab "brothers." Instead, the Moroccan independence movement rejected both French and Spanish presence in North Africa. Spain's support of the anti-French struggle also failed to earn it special consideration in postcolonial negotiations. In fact, Moroccans privileged French interests over Spanish interests after attaining independence. The loss of Morocco may not have upset Franco as it did some of his hard-line supporters; the caudillo was undoubtedly astute enough to regard it as inevitable. But his government was not particularly pleased by the lack of Moroccan gratitude for its earlier support against the French and the "civilizing" efforts it had made in the protectorate.

Spain continued to retain some North African territory after 1956, thereby preserving imperial pride and giving many military officers a sense of mission. In addition to Ceuta and Melilla, which remain Spanish to this day, Spain retained the Sidi Ifni enclave on Morocco's Atlantic coast and the larger areas of Cabo Juby and the Western Sahara to the south. Franco considered all of these territories to constitute Spanish soil, and he ordered his military forces to continue to occupy them. In addition, Spanish forces remained in the coastal region around Tarfaya, which served as a buffer zone to the northwest corner of the Western Sahara. They also retained defensive positions in the mountains surrounding Melilla until 1960.

The Western Sahara proved particularly problematic for the Spanish military. In the summer of 1957 the Army for the Liberation of the Sahara, fighting in the name of Moroccan territorial expansion, attacked French posts in Algeria and Mauritania. Because Spain lacked enough troops to fight effectively, its generals preferred not to get involved. As a result, their territory became

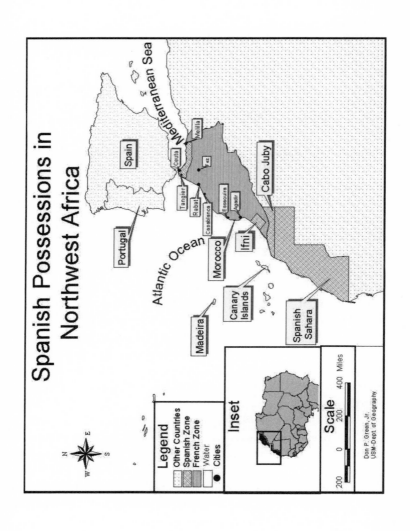

Spanish Possessions in Northwest Africa

Mediterranean Sea

Spain

Portugal

Ceuta
Melilla
Tangier
Rabat
Casablanca
Fez
Essaouira
Agadir

Atlantic Ocean

Morocco

Ifni

Cabo Juby

Madeira

Canary Islands

Spanish Sahara

Legend

- Other Countries
- Spanish Zone
- French Zone
- Water
- Cities ●

N
E
W
S

Inset

Scale

200   0   200   400 Miles

Don P. Green, Jr.
USM-Dept. of Geography

a safe haven for Moroccan forces fighting the French. But French troops entered the Spanish area in pursuit of the Moroccans, thereby pulling the Spaniards into the conflict.

The Army for the Liberation of the Sahara then invaded Ifni in what some officers in Spain came to refer to wryly as "the forgotten war." After three days Spanish forces halted the invasion but in the process lost sixty-two men. The Moroccans struck again near El Aaiun, this time causing 241 Spanish deaths before finally being stopped with the help of air strikes and French support. The Spaniards eventually retreated to a defensive parameter around the town of Sidi Ifni, where they would remain for the next twelve years. Spanish forces managed to regain control of much of the Sahara with the support of the French, who wanted to prevent Morocco from expanding into Mauritania to the south. Although Franco agreed to relinquish Cabo Juby in early 1958, he remained adamant about keeping Ifni and the Sahara, elevating both to the status of Spanish provinces. Farther to the south, Spain continued to hold on to the West African territory that would become Equatorial Guinea.[6]

On mainland Spain the army also remained at least somewhat occupied by military threats. Beginning in 1944, armed Communists based in France crossed the northwest border of Spain on several occasions with the intention of waging guerrilla warfare. The largest postwar incursion forces, which crossed the Pyrenees Mountains in the direction of the Lerida province, may have numbered as many as 4,000. But they passed through the Vall d'Aran, an area characterized in part by Catalan nationalism but also by conservative Catholicism, where the Communists failed to gain much popular support. Francoist military and police forces had little trouble stopping these invaders and other, smaller-scale guerrilla attacks before they posed a significant threat.

In addition to the Communists, anarchist guerrillas managed to make isolated attacks in Spain until the early 1950s, mostly in mountainous areas. In 1945 they also launched a brief attack on the local Falange headquarters in the Cuatro Caminos district of

Madrid. In Barcelona several gunfights took place between anarchists and government forces in 1948 and 1949, but the anarchist threat, never very significant, had disappeared by the 1950s. In a sense, the guerrilla attacks served Franco well. They never posed a genuine danger to his rule, but the apparent leftist threat to public order and security helped him justify the persistence of military law.[7]

Yet in other ways the entrenched conservatism that the colonial and antiguerrilla campaigns fostered made things more difficult for the regime. Because of the persistence of an antimodern, civil war–era mindset in so many influential circles, Spaniards who sought to reform the country's more antiquated institutions and practices had a particularly hard time. Some officers even protested that the 1953 agreement with the United States posed a threat to the very essence of the Spanish military, arguing that it replaced the army's traditional spiritual and warrior values with an overemphasis on technology and foreign ideas.[8] In the sphere of economics, moreover, the traditionalist resistance to economic modernization was even more problematic.

Initially, Franco tried to deal with the economic hardship after the civil war with what has been called "a solid military logic," including government controls on prices and industry.[9] The dictatorship pursued a policy of limited autarky, or economic self-sufficiency, and kept Spain largely out of the international market. Such a policy did not prove helpful in a country suffering from falling real wages, droughts, very weak industrial and agricultural production, and considerable poverty. To this day, surviving Spaniards still refer to this period as the "years of hunger." Although conditions improved considerably in the 1950s, some hard-line resistance to changes in economic policy persisted. When a group of Spaniards tried to bring about a partial democratic opening of the Spanish economy in 1962, the Francoist hard-liners condemned their endeavors as treasonous.

By the late 1950s, however, Franco had brought civilians more friendly to free-market capitalism into his government. Known as the technocrats, many were members of Opus Dei, a Catholic lay organization. Thereafter, Spain's financial health began to improve, aided by growing foreign investment, some industrialization, and a rise in tourist revenues. In addition, many Spanish workers in places like Switzerland, Germany, and Great Britain sent part of their income to families back home, thereby contributing further to Spain's economy. But the modernization of the economy also had its enemies, especially among some of the more radical members of the Falange and the same ultraconservative monarchists whom they had earlier opposed. In their view, the new, liberal economic practices espoused by the Opus Dei technocrats threatened the traditional values of Nationalist Spain. The appearance of nongovernmental workers' organizations and labor strikes also caused concern.

Moreover, military officers and Falangists reacted very strongly to small but increasingly frequent acts of terrorism. Understandably, Franco shared their reaction, and he was especially disturbed that much of the terrorism took place at the hands of ETA (in English, Basque Homeland and Liberty), a Basque nationalist organization. As we have seen, Franco grew up with a strong dislike of separatism and anything he believed to threaten Spanish unity, including Freemasonry and socialism. In his view, the loss of Spanish colonies in 1898 and the violent disorder of the 1909 Tragic Week in Barcelona had made clear the dangers of separatist movements. Now it seemed as if separatism might again prove a serious threat. Although the Catalan nationalist leaders generally rejected violence, some of their Basque counterparts were willing to support ETA's actions.

In 1968, during a time of increasingly troublesome protests by workers and Basque nationalists, ETA assassinated the head of the political police in Guipúzcoa, one of the Basque provinces. Many more assassinations have followed this one, ETA's first, in a terrorist campaign that has persisted into the early twenty-first century. The Guipúzcoa killing was a response to the murder of two ETA members by police, and in its immediate wake, the government arrested almost 2,000 ETA members and suspected supporters and broadened the jurisdiction of military courts.

Some of the imprisoned were tortured and even killed by Spanish security forces.

Franco decided to allow several of the jailed ETA members to be tried in public. Their trial, in Burgos in December 1970, was an international public relations disaster for the caudillo. European community leaders joined the pope in urging Franco to be lenient, and an old Basque veteran of the civil war attracted attention by setting himself on fire and jumping from a building in San Sebastian as Franco passed by. On 28 December nine of the defendants received the death sentence. Although Franco commuted the sentences to life imprisonment three days later, his enemies nonetheless succeeded in drawing negative attention to the dictatorship. Thanks to the Burgos trial, moreover, ETA's prestige rose among many Basques. Between the first killing and 1975, ETA claimed forty-seven victims, losing about thirty of its own to the police. Even if many Spaniards did not particularly mind Franco's repression of Basque (and Catalan) separatism, his heavy-handed approach proved counterproductive overall, and many people suffered or lost their lives at the hands of his forces.[10]

ETA's most famous assassination, which had tremendous consequences for the regime and for Spain as a whole, profoundly affected Franco on both personal and political levels. The victim, Adm. Luis Carrero Blanco, was Franco's most intimate and faithful collaborator, and the caudillo had intended for him to play a crucial role in ensuring the future of the dictatorship. Carrero Blanco had first met Franco during the Moroccan war of the 1920s, and during the civil war he had served in the Nationalist navy. After the war Franco had made him chief of naval operations on the admiralty's staff, and in 1951 he had charged Carrero Blanco with coordinating the policies of Spain's different ministries. Given Franco's tendency to keep the powers below him divided, the decision to give Carrero Blanco influence over intergovernmental relationships reflected a considerable amount of trust.

In 1966 Carrero reached the rank of admiral, and Franco appointed him premier in June 1973, signaling the first time that anyone other than Franco himself had held the position during the dictatorship. Carrero Blanco's appointment stemmed from Franco's belief that filling this crucial post with someone who shared his views could guarantee the preservation of Spain's extreme right-wing character even after the caudillo's death. Franco may have had already expressed his confidence that Spain's future was "well secured" (*bien atado*), but he nevertheless wanted to be certain that the dictatorship's most important institutions would live on as he believed they should.

Because ETA knew Carrero Blanco was so important for Spain's future, it targeted him in a spectacular, carefully planned and executed assassination. After considerable efforts to dig a tunnel and place electrically detonated explosives under the street, on the morning of 20 December 1973, an ETA squad set off a huge blast under Carrero Blanco's car as he drove to Mass. The explosion was so great that the car landed on the fourth-floor roof of the church and Jesuit monastery across the street, not far from the U.S. Embassy. Carrero Blanco, his driver, and a police escort were all killed instantly.

Almost immediately, the effects of the assassination spread across Spain. Fearing the regime's reaction, the Communist Party and other workers' organizations promptly cancelled their planned illegal demonstrations. The Communist leaders also went out of their way to convey that they had played no role in the killing. Fortunately, Spain remained calm, even as the military went on alert and the ETA squad escaped to Portugal and then France.

Carrero Blanco's funeral made painfully apparent the impact of the assassination on Franco. Although he had managed to guard his emotions remarkably well for most of his life, during the memorial service he broke down in tears. Television cameras captured the moment as the eighty-one-year-old Franco, suffering from the onset of Parkinson's disease, projected a dramatically different image than he had as the triumphant *generalísimo* of the civil war decades earlier.

In the meantime, the European protest movements of the late

1960s had begun to appear in Spain, financial scandals reached high into the government, and the country continued to lose its hold on its overseas possessions. In October 1968 Equatorial Guinea gained independence from Spain, and the Franco regime's relations with the new African state turned into such a diplomatic disaster that in 1972 the Spanish government banned all news about Guinea.[11] In the Western Sahara, moreover, Spain soon lost even more of its colonial territory while a dying Franco watched, powerless to halt the process.

Known as the *Frente Polisario*, the Western Sahara's independence movement sought to end Spanish occupation but was equally adamant in its refusal to be swallowed up by Morocco. In September 1973 Franco promised to grant the people of the Sahara the right to decide their own political sovereignty sometime in the future, although he did not specify when. The Moroccan king, Hassan II, who found the issue an effective way to increase his popularity at home, repeatedly pushed his claim that the area belonged to Morocco, drawing the United Nations into the fray. Although the International Court eventually ruled that the people of the Sahara had the right to self-determination, King Hassan garnered significant support on the issue not only within Morocco, but from many Arab governments and, ironically enough, the PLO.[12]

In Spain Franco continued to adhere to his life-long principles even in the face of intense international pressure, approving the execution in September 1975 of five terrorists, while commuting the sentences of six others. Massive demonstrations broke out all over Europe in protest, although they had scant effect on Franco. Yet his health continued to deteriorate, and in the meantime, King Hassan announced that he would order a "Green March" of hundreds of thousands of Moroccans into the Western Sahara. On 6 November the Green March began. The Spanish military did not fire on the massive group of invading civilians, thereby averting bloodshed. One week later, Spain agreed to withdraw from the Sahara, a far from glorious ending to Spain's last sizable overseas territory. After the Spanish withdrawal, the *Polisario* continued to wage guerrilla warfare against Moroccan forces until a 1991 UN-brokered ceasefire. Thereafter, despite high-level efforts by the United States and UN mediation, the status of the Sahara remained unsettled, and in the early twenty-first century more than 100,000 saharawis still lived in refugee camps across the Algerian border.

Meanwhile, a dying Franco granted interim rule to Prince Juan Carlos on 13 November 1975. After enduring several operations and horrible pain with considerable stoicism, the caudillo died on 20 November. As Franco had decided, Juan Carlos assumed the title of King of Spain. In opposition to the caudillo's wishes, however, the new king soon revealed that he favored democratic reforms. In July 1976 the king appointed a new premier, Adolfo Suárez González, who initiated the process that eventually brought democracy back to Spain.

After Franco's death, Spain departed markedly from the path the caudillo had intended it to take. But in life he had achieved many of his goals, both for his country and for himself. His conservative military mind, while not that of a genius, had served him well. From his modest origins in El Ferrol, Franco had risen to the status of military hero in North Africa, the victorious commander in chief of a hard-fought war, and one of modern history's longest-ruling dictators.

He ruled ruthlessly at times, at the cost of tens of thousands of lives. According to his defenders, he nonetheless merits praise for halting Spain's fall into violent disorder. Defenders argue that without the restoration of order that Franco achieved, Spain could never have developed into the modern, stable, and prosperous state it is now, and in fact, in many ways the country was in far better shape after being ruled by Franco than it had been at the start of the civil war. In the diplomatic sphere, the Franco regime took credit for keeping Spain out of World War II, the 1953 base treaty with the United States, the entry into the United Nations in 1955, and the country's membership in the World Bank, the International Monetary Fund, and the Organization for Economic Cooperation and Development beginning in 1958.

In reality, though, Franco himself was not responsible for many of the dictatorship's triumphs after the civil war, some of which resulted from pure luck or even stood in opposition to his values. Had it been possible, Franco would have joined forces with Hitler in World War II, believing for much of the conflict that Nazi Germany would emerge victorious. During the cold war, he benefited greatly from international circumstances well beyond his control, although he was astute enough to make them work to his advantage. He lacked a full understanding of many of the economic and social changes Spain underwent during his dictatorship, and some developments occurred in spite of his leadership and not because of it. After World War II Spaniards lacked many basic freedoms that most western Europeans took for granted. Corruption, nepotism, and favoritism were widespread, and Franco's extensive and harsh repression of his opponents produced so much bloodshed that it shocked even some of his allies, although one may question whether a victory by some of the leftist forces in Spain would have been any better.

Above all, Franco understood how to take advantage of opportunities when they arose. His natural caution and conservatism proved particularly valuable during the civil war, as did the lessons he took from years of service in Morocco. He knew how to manage the various institutions and interests below him while maintaining the stability of his regime. In the end, his identity as a soldier did much to shape the course and character of his dictatorship.

Notes

Chapter 1

1. The following biographical information comes primarily from Paul Preston, *Franco: A Biography* (New York: BasicBooks, 1994), 1–9, and Stanley G. Payne, *The Franco Regime, 1936–1939* (Madison: University of Wisconsin Press, 1987), 67–70.

2. Ricardo de la Cierva, *Franco* (Barcelona, Planeta: 1986), 26–30; Sheelagh Ellwood, *Franco* (London: Longman, 1994), 3; Gabrielle Ashford Hodges, *Franco: A Concise Biography* (New York: Thomas Dunne, 2000), 23; Gabriel Cardona, *Franco no estudió en West Point* (Barcelona: Littera, 2002), 21–22.

3. Antonio García Pérez, *Consejos á los caballeros alumnos de la Academia de Infantería* (Toledo, [1910]), 10–11.

4. Carlos Fernández, *El general Franco* (Barcelona: Argos Vergara, 1983), 17; Payne, *Franco Regime*, 69–70; Preston, *Franco*, 9–10.

5. *Reglamento provisional para la instrucción táctica de las tropas de infantería* (Madrid, 1908), 124.

6. Francisco Franco Bahamonde, *Papeles de la guerra de Marruecos* (Madrid: Fundación Francisco Franco, 1986), 43–44.

7. George Hills, *Franco: The Man and his Nation* (New York: Macmillan, 1967), 63–64.

8. *Reglamento provisional para la instrucción de tiro con ametralladoras de infantería* (Madrid, 1911); *Táctica para columnas de desembarco de los buques con arreglo al Reglamento táctico de Infantería* (Madrid, 1913).

9. El Capitán Equis [Nazario Cebreiros], *El problema militar en España: Apuntes para un estudio sincero y al alcance de todos*, vol. 2 (Burgos, 1917), 41–103.

10. Geoffrey Jensen, *Irrational Triumph: Cultural Despair, Military Nationalism, and the Ideological Origins of Franco's Spain* (Reno: University of Nevada Press, 2002), 63–64, 149–51.

11. See Carolyn P. Boyd, *Praetorian Politics in Liberal Spain* (Chapel Hill: University of North Carolina Press, 1979). A revised Spanish edition of this book has been published as *La política pretoriana en al reinado de Alfonso XIII*, trans. Mauro Hernández Benítez (Madrid: Alianza, 1990).

Chapter 2

1. Cierva, *Franco*, 37; Preston, *Franco*, 19.

2. José Álvarez, *The Betrothed of Death: The Spanish Foreign Legion During the Rif Rebellion, 1920–1927* (Westport, Conn.: Greenwood, 2001), 1; Ellwood, *Franco*, 11.

3. Sebastian Balfour, *Deadly Embrace: Morocco and the Road to the Spanish Civil War* (Oxford: Oxford University Press, 2002), 6, 16–23; C. R. Pennell, *A Country with a Government and a Flag: The Rif War in Morocco, 1921–1926*, 22–23; C. R. Pennell, *Morocco since 1830* (New York: New York University Press, 2000), 28, 304–305.

4. Carlos Martínez de Campos y Serrano, *Ayer: 1892–1931* (Madrid: Instituto de Estudios Politicos, 1946), 72–73, 57–59, 82–84.

5. Franco, *Papeles*, 32, 59, 176–78.

6. Boyd, *Praetorian*, 20–22.

7. Cierva, *Franco*, 36.

8. Balfour, *Deadly Embrace*, 23–25; Cierva, *Franco*, 36.

9. Preston, *Franco*, 16.

10. Quoted in Álvarez, *Betrothed*, 6.

11. Boyd, *Praetorian*, 40–41.

12. Javier Tusell, *Franco en la Guerra Civil. Una biografía política* (Barcelona: Tusquets, 1992), 16.

13. Gabriel Cardona, "El joven Franco, como se forja un dictador," *Clio. El pasado presente* (Feb. 2003) 18–25; Enrique Moradiellos, *Francisco Franco: Crónica de un caudillo casi olvidado* (Madrid: Biblioteca Nueva, 2002), 265.

14. Álvarez, *Betrothed*, 8.

15. Balfour, *Deadly Embrace*, 40–41.

16. On El Raisuni and the Spaniards during this period, Balfour, *Deadly Embrace*, 41, 33–35; Pennell, *Morocco*, 127; Shannon E. Fleming, *Primo de Rivera and Abd-el-Krim: The Struggle for Spanish Morocco, 1923–1927* (New York: Garland, 1991), 40; Pennell, *Country*, 46.

17. Preston, *Franco*, 14; Álvarez, *Betrothed*, 4; Cierva, *Franco*, 41.

18. Preston, *Franco*, 17–18; Cierva, *Franco*, 42–44; Álvarez, *Betrothed*, 37–38; Franco, *Papeles*, 35–37; Payne, *Franco Regime*, 70.

19. Preston, *Franco*, 18–19; Payne, *Franco Regime*, 71.

20. Preston, *Franco*, 21, 24.

21. Brian Bond, "The Somme in British History," in *War in the Age of Technology: Myriad Faces of Modern Armed Conflict*, eds. Geoffrey Jensen and Andrew Wiest (New York: New York University Press, 2001), 194–210.

22. Franco, *Papeles*, 43–44.

Chapter 3

1. Preston, *Franco*, 28.

2. José Millán-Astray, *La Legión*, 2nd ed. (Madrid, 1980); Richard Sablotny, *Legionnaire in Morocco* (Los Angeles: Wetzel, 1940), 117; Preston, *Franco*, 29.

3. "Paraphrase of Cablegram Received," from U.S. Consulate General, 20 Nov. 1921, Madrid; and Major R. B. Cocroft, U.S. Military Attaché, Madrid, to Major M. Churchill, Chief, Military Intelligence Division, Washington, D.C., 25 Jan. 1922. Both documents are in National Archives and Records Administration, Washington, D.C., Correspondence of the Military Intelligence Division Relating to General, Political, Economic, and Military Conditions in Spain, 1918–1941 (hereafter NARA Military Intelligence).

4. Millán-Astray, *Legión*, 16, 21–22. María Rosa de Madariaga, *Los moros que trajo Franco . . . : La intervención de tropas coloniales en la Guerra Civil* (Madrid: Martínez Roca, 2002), 80–81, 95; Fernández, *General Franco*, 71; Preston, *Franco*, 29–30; Payne, *Franco Regime*, 71–72n. 11.

5. Boyd, *Política pretoriana,* 200; Gabriel Cardona, *El poder militar en la España contemporánea hasta la guerra civil* (Madrid: Alianza, 1983), 71; Pennell, *Morocco*, 188.

6. Balfour, *Deadly Embrace*, 60–61; Pennell, *Country*, 22.

7. Boyd, *Praetorian*, 287; Franco, *Papeles,* 77. This part of *Papeles* is a reprint of Franco's *Diario de una Bandera* (Madrid, 1922).

8. Álvarez, *Betrothed,* 41.

9. Pennell, *Morocco,* 190; Álvarez, *Betrothed,* 43–44.

10. Álvarez, *Betrothed,* 45–51.

11. Cited in Álvarez, *Betrothed,* 52, and Preston, *Franco,* 32.

12. Preston, *Franco,* 32–33.

13. Boyd, *Política pretoriana*, 208, 232, 253–57; Fernández, *General Franco*, 30.

14. Emilio Mola Vidal, *El pasado, Azaña y el porvenir: Las tragedias de nuestras instituciones militares* (Madrid: Imp. Sáez, 1934), 254–57.

15. Boyd, *Política pretoriana*, 268–70; Preston, *Franco*, 35, 41–45; Pennell, *Country,* 166–70.

16. Balfour, *Deadly Embrace,* 61. This account of the 1924 Spanish withdrawal is drawn primarily from Álvarez, *Betrothed,* 122–41, and Balfour, *Deadly Embrace,* 95–105.

17. Franco, *Papeles,* 189–95. (This selection was originally published in 1926).

18. Stanley G. Payne, *Politics and the Military in Modern Spain* (Stanford: Stanford University Press, 1967), 213–14.

19. On the Al Hoceima Bay landing and its immediate antecedents, José E. Álvarez, "Between Gallipoli and D-Day: Alhucemas, 1925," *Journal of Military History* 63, no.1 (Jan. 1999): 75–98; Balfour, *Deadly Embrace*, 108–12; and Fleming, *Primo de Rivera,* 263–99.

20. Franco, *Papeles,* 205–206. Franco's description of the Al Hoceima landing first appeared in *Revista de Tropas Coloniales* (Sept.–Dec. 1925). It is also reproduced in Fernández, *General Franco,* 293–95.

21. Preston, *Franco,* 48.

22. Balfour, *Deadly Embrace,* 112.

23. Juan Pablo Fusí, *Franco: Autoritarismo y poder personal* (Barcelona: Suma de Letras, 2001), 42.

24. Jensen, *Irrational Triumph,* 68–69, 121; Mola, *Azaña,* 132–33; Preston, *Franco,* 59.

Chapter 4

1. Payne, *Franco Regime,* 76.

2. Preston, *Franco,* 79.

3. Tusell, *Franco*, 18.
4. For example, the 19 June 1968 journal entry of Max Aub, reprinted in "¿De qué le sirvió la República?" *El País*, "Babelia" section (31 May 2003), 3.
5. Carlos Martínez de Campos, *Ayer: segunda parte, 1931–1953* (Madrid: Instituto de Estudio Politicos, 1970), 21.
6. Mola, *El pasado*.
7. Preston, *Franco*, 80–81.
8. Tusell, *Franco*, 15–19; Payne, *Franco Regime*, 76–78.
9. Ellwood, *Franco*, 55. On the previous anarchist insurrections during the Republic, Stanley G. Payne, *Spain's First Democracy: The Second Republic, 1931–1939* (Madison: University of Wisconsin Press, 1993), 52–57, 127–34.
10. Preston, *Franco*, 101–104.
11. Martínez de Campos, *Ayer: segunda parte*, 29–39. On the military aspects of the Asturian revolt, see Payne, *Spain's First Democracy*, 218–23.
12. Preston, *Franco*, 104–105; Payne, *Spain's First Democracy*, 430n. 65.
13. On Franco and Spain in Feb.–July 1936, Tusell, *Franco*, 19–30, and Payne, *Franco Regime*, 91–94.
14. Payne, *Politics*, 342; Tusell, *Franco*, 32, 141; Jean Grugel and Tim Rees, *Franco's Spain* (London: Arnold, 1997), 13.

Chapter 5
1. Payne, *Franco Regime*, 123–26.
2. Preston, *Franco*, 165.
3. Francisco Espinosa, *La columna de la muerte: el avance del ejército franquista de Sevilla a Badajoz* (Barcelona: Crítica, 2003), 56.
4. Espinosa, *Columna*, 72–77, 205–43.
5. José Andrés-Gallego and Antón M. Pazos, eds., *Archivo Gomá. Documentos de la Guerra Civil*, vol. 1, July–Dec. 1936 (Madrid: Consejo Superior de Investigaciones Científicas, 2001), 227–28.
6. Balfour, *Deadly Embrace*, 168; Michael Alpert, *El ejército republicano en la guerra civil*, 2nd ed. (Madrid: Siglo XXI, 1989), 331–35; Fernández, *General Franco*, 72–73.
7. Fernández, *General Franco*, 73.
8. Alpert, *El ejército*, 338–41; Payne, *Franco Regime*, 198.
9. *Normas de orientación reguladoras de la actuación del mando de división* (Burgos: Jefatura de Movilización, Instrucción y Recuperación, 1938); Payne, *Franco Regime*, 209–10.

10. Quoted in Espinosa, *Columna*, 14.

11. James W. Cortada, ed., *A City in War: American Views on Barcelona and the Spanish Civil War, 1936–1939* (Wilmington, Del.: Scholarly Resources, 1985), 164–65; Mark A. Clodfelter, "Molding Airpower Convictions: Development and Legacy of William Mitchell's Strategic Thought," in *Paths of Heaven*, ed. Phillip S. Meilinger (Maxwell AFB: Air University Press, 1997), 96.

12. Translated report of French military intelligence staff officer, submitted by Lt. Col. Sumner Waite (U.S. assistant military attaché), Paris, Report 23,106-W, 18 January 1937, NARA Military Intelligence, 2657-S-144-86.; Lt. Col. Raymond E. Lee (U.S. military attaché), London, Report 38512, 25 January 1937, NARA Military Intelligence, 2657-S-144-88.

13. Col. Stephen O. Fuqua (U.S. military attaché), Madrid, Report 6441, 19 December 1936, NARA Military Intelligence, 2657-S-144-77.

14. Andrés-Gallego and Pazos, *Archivo Gomá*, 180–81; Preston, *Franco*, 181.

15. On the Soviet military contribution, see Daniel Kowalsky, *La Unión Soviética y la Guerra Civil Española* (Barcelona: Crítica, 2003), chapters 10–17.

16. Waite, Report 23,106-W, 18 January 1937; Miguel Alonso Baquer, "Características militares de Franco," in *Franco y su época*, ed. Luis Suárez Fernández (Madrid: ACTAS, 1993), 17–38.

17. Waite, Report 23,106-W, 18 January 1937.

18. Payne, *Franco Regime*, 126–31; Gabriel Cardona, "La batalla de Madrid," in *La Guerra Civil*, vol. 9 (Madrid: Historia 16), 38–43; Antony Beevor, *Spanish Civil War* (New York: Penguin, 2001), 155; Judith Keene, *Fighting for Franco: International Volunteers in Nationalist Spain during the Spanish Civil War, 1936–39* (London: Leicester University Press, 2001), 125.

19. Preston, *Franco*, 229–35; Payne, *Franco*, 131–43; Tusell, *Franco*, 110–14.

20. U.S. military attaché, Barcelona, Report 6761, 26 January 1938, NARA Military Intelligence, 2657-S-144-327.

21. Cortada, *City*, 125–73; Ángel Bahamonde Magro and Javier Cervera Gil, *Así terminó la Guerra de España* (Madrid: Marcial Pons, 2000), 93–94, 148–60.

22. Michael Alpert, "La historia militar," in *La guerra civil: una nueva vision del conflict que dividió España*, eds. Stanley G. Payne and Javier Tusell (Madrid: Temas de Hoy, 1996), 123–224; Bahamonde and Cervera, *Así terminó*, 38–44.
23. Edward N. Luttwak, *Strategy: The Logic of War and Peace* (Cambridge: Harvard University Press, 2001), 92; Wallace P. Franz, "Two Letters on Strategy: Clausewitz' Contribution to the Operational Level of War," in *Clausewitz and Modern Strategy*, ed. Michael I. Handel (London: Cass, 1986), 171–94; Stephen Ashley Hart, *Montgomery and "Colossal Cracks": The 21st Army Group in Europe, 1944–45* (Westport, Conn.: Praeger, 2000), 12–14; Archer Jones, *The Art of Warfare in the Western World* (Urbana and Chicago: University of Illinois Press, 1987), 1, 55.
24. Juan Benet, "Tres fechas. Sobre la estrategía en la Guerra Civil Española," in *La sombra de la guerra: Escritos sobre la Guerra Civil Española* (Madrid: Taurus, 1999), 145–72.
25. Alistair Horne, *To Lose a Battle: France, 1940* (London: Macmillan, 1969); Ernest R. May, *Strange Victory: Hitler's Conquest of France* (New York: Hill and Wang, 2000).
26. Luttwak, *Strategy*, 90n; David M. Glantz, *Soviet Military Operational Art: In Pursuit of Deep Battle* (London: Frank Cass, 1991), 16–24; Niall J. A. Barr, "The Elusive Victory: The BEF and the Operational Level of War, September 1918," in *War in the Age of Technology*, eds. Jensen and Wiest, 213–14.
27. Mary R. Habeck, *Storm of Steel: The Development of Armor Doctrine in Germany and the Soviet Union, 1919–1939* (Ithaca, NY: Cornell University Press, 2003), 257–62
28. Gen. Galera Paniagua, prologue to *Papeles*, by Franco, 11; Michael Seidman, *Republic of Egos: A Social History of the Spanish Civil War* (Madison: University of Wisconsin Press, 2002).
29. *Normas*.
30. Mathew Hughes and Enriquetta Garrido, "Planning and Command: The Spanish Republican Army and the Battle of the Ebro," *International Journal of Iberian Studies* 12:2 (1999): 97–115; Alpert, "Historia militar"; Steven J. Zaloga, "Soviet Tank Operations in the Spanish Civil War," *Journal of Slavic Military Studies* 12, no. 3 (Sept. 1990): 134–62; Stanley G. Payne, *Unión*

Soviética, comunismo y revolución en España (1931–1939)
(Madrid: Plaza Janés, 2003), 220–27.

31. Payne, *Franco Regime*, 99–100; Carolyn P. Boyd, "Las reformas militares," in *Historia General de España y América*, vol. XVII, *La Segunda República y la Guerra* (Madrid: Rialp, 1996), 171.

Chapter 6

1. Antonio Cazorla, *Las políticas de la victoria: la consolidación del Nuevo Estado franquista, 1938–1953* (Madrid: Marcial Pons, 2000), 98–103; Payne, *Franco Regime*, 209–28; Preston, *Franco*, 226–27.
2. Payne, *Franco Regime*, 313–42.
3. Wayne H. Bowen, *Spaniards and Nazi Germany: Collaboration in the New Order* (Columbia: University of Missouri Press, 2000), 99–101.
4. Payne, *Franco Regime*, 328–32.
5. Paul Preston, "Decay, Division, and the Defence of Dictatorship: The Military and Politics, 1939–1975," in *Élites and Power in Twentieth-Century Spain. Essays in Honour of Sir Raymond Carr*, eds. Frances Lannon and Paul Preston (Oxford: Clarendon Press, 1990), 205–209; Grugel and Rees, *Franco's Spain*, 52–53; Payne, *Franco Regime*, 242–45.
6. Concepción Ybarra, "El final del Protectorado. Descolonización," *Aventura de la Historia* 50 (Dec. 2002): 48–53; Pennell, *Morocco*, 293–94, 301–302; Payne, *Franco Regime*, 429–30.
7. Payne, *Franco Regime*, 345–46, 378.
8. Juan Carlos Losada Malvárez, *Ideología del Ejército Franquista 1939–1959* (Madrid: Istmo, 1990), 56–59.
9. Grugel and Rees, *Franco's Spain*, 106.
10. Payne, *Franco Regime*, 558–60.
11. Xavier Lacosta, "España-Guinea, 1969–1976: acercamientos y alejamientos," *Historia 16* XXVII, no. 325 (May 2003): 90–103.
12. Pennell, *Morocco*, 336–40; Payne, *Franco Regime*, 612–13.

Bibliographic Note

FORTUNATELY for English-language readers who wish to learn more about Franco, some of the most important works about the late dictator were first published in the United States and Great Britain. Paul Preston's massive book, *Franco: A Biography* (New York: BasicBooks, 1994), is an engaging critical biography by a leading historian of modern Spain. Stanley G. Payne's excellent account of the caudillo and the political history of Spain under his rule, *The Franco Regime, 1936–1939* (Madison: University of Wisconsin Press, 1987), includes meaningful comparative analysis of Franco, the civil war, and the dictatorship in an international context, unlike far too many other works of Spanish history. Juan Pablo Fusí's *Franco: A Biography* (New York: Harper & Row, 1987) has much thoughtful discussion of Franco's personality, politics, and rule, although the latest edition of the book has not been translated into English [*Franco: Autoritarismo y poder personal* (Barcelona: Suma de Letras, 2001)]. *Franco's Spain* (London: Arnold, 1997) by Jean Grugel and Tim Rees is a relatively brief but very good introduction to the dictatorship, focusing more on the regime in its many dimensions than on Franco himself.

Other English-language biographies of Franco include Sheelagh Ellwood, *Franco* (Essex: Longman, 1994); George Hills, *Franco: The Man and his Nation* (New York: Macmillan, 1967);

and Gabrielle Ashford Hodges, *Franco* (New York: Thomas Dunne, 2000). The latter is a compelling but often speculative interpretation, subjecting Franco to the kind of intense psychological analysis from which few historical figures could probably emerge unscathed. Of the above three historians, only Hills, a former British army officer, shows a deep interest in military affairs, but his book accepts the Francoist version of many developments too readily.

On the military in general in twentieth-century Spain, Stanley G. Payne's *Politics and the Military in Modern Spain* (Stanford: Stanford University Press, 1967) remains an important and useful work. The tumultuous political and military context of Franco's service as a young officer is analyzed in depth by Carolyn P. Boyd in *Praetorian Politics in Liberal Spain* (Chapel Hill: University of North Carolina Press, 1979). Although a later version of this book exists only in Spanish [*La política pretoriana en el reinado de Alfonso XIII* (Madrid: Alianza, 1990)], the original edition is now available on the web site of *LIBRO: The Library of Iberian Resources Online* (http://libro.uca.edu). Paul Preston's *The Politics of Revenge: Fascism and the Military in Twentieth-Century Spain* (New York: Routledge, 1995) focuses above all on the political history of the military and Franco, whereas Geoffrey Jensen's *Irrational Triumph: Cultural Despair, Military Nationalism, and the Ideological Origins of Franco's Spain* (Reno: University of Nevada Press, 2002), explores the nationalist, cultural, and philosophical dimensions of the environment that produced Franco.

Spain's military campaigns in North Africa are covered in Sebastian Balfour, *Deadly Embrace: Morocco and the Road to the Spanish Civil War* (Oxford: Oxford University Press, 2002); Shannon E. Fleming, *Primo de Rivera and Abd-el-Krim: The Struggle for Spanish Morocco, 1923–1927* (New York: Garland, 1991); C. R. Pennell, *A Country with a Government and a Flag: The Rif War in Morocco, 1921–1926* (Cambridgeshire, U.K.: Middle East and North African Studies Press, 1986); and Robert Woolman, *Rebels in the Rif* (Stanford: Stanford University Press,

1968). José Álvarez's *The Betrothed of Death: The Spanish Foreign Legion During the Rif Rebellion, 1920–1927* (Westport, Conn.: Greenwood, 2001) examines the Legion's military operations during a key period in its history and Franco's military career.

Books on the Second Republic and civil war with extensive discussion of Franco include Michael Alpert, *A New International History of the Spanish Civil War* (New York: St. Martin's, 1994); Antony Beevor, *The Spanish Civil War* (New York: Penguin, 2001); George Esenwein and Adrian Shubert, *Spain at War: The Spanish Civil War in Context, 1931–1939* (London: Longman, 1995); Gabriel Jackson, *The Spanish Republic and Civil War, 1931–1939* (Princeton: Princeton University Press, 1965); Paul Preston, *The Spanish Civil War, 1936–1939* (London: Weidenfeld and Nicolson, 1986); and Hugh Thomas, *The Spanish Civil War*, rev. ed. (New York: Modern Library, 2001). A short account in English of one of most important battles of the war is Chris Henry's *The Ebro 1938: Death Knell of the Republic* (Oxford: Osprey, 1999). English-language readers also have access to an on-line edition of Daniel Kowalsky's *The Soviet Union and the Spanish Republic: Diplomatic, Military, and Cultural Relations, 1936–1939*, published by Columbia University Press [http://www.gutenberg-e.org; Spanish ed., *La Unión Soviética y la Guerra Civil Española* (Barcelona: Crítica, 2003)].

By necessity, this brief essay omits many other noteworthy books on Franco and modern Spanish history in general. For further reading, including titles in Spanish and other languages not included here, see the bibliographies of Payne, Preston, Thomas, Alpert, and Esenwein and Shubert.

About the Author

Geoffrey Jensen is the author of *Irrational Triumph: Cultural Despair, Military Nationalism, and the Ideological Origins of Franco's Spain* (2002), and coeditor, with Andrew Wiest, of *War in the Age of Technology: Myriad Faces of Modern Armed Conflict* (2001). He has taught at Yale, UCLA, the University of Southern Mississippi, and the Royal Military Academy Sandhurst, and he now holds the John C. Biggs '30 Cincinnati Chair in Military History at the Virginia Military Institute.

MILITARY PROFILES
AVAILABLE

Farragut: America's First Admiral
Robert J. Scneller Jr.
Drake: For God, Queen, and Plunder
Wade G. Dudley
Santa Anna: A Curse Upon Mexico
Robert L. Scheina
Eisenhower: Soldier-Statesman of the American Century
Douglas Kinnard
Semmes: Rebel Raider
John M. Taylor
Doolittle: Aerospace Visionary
Dik Alan Daso
Foch: Supreme Allied Commander in the Great War
Michael S. Neiberg
Villa: Soldier of the Mexican Revolution
Robert L. Scheina
Cushing: Civil War SEAL
Robert J. Schneller, Jr.
Alexander the Great: Invincible King of Macedonia
Peter G. Tsouras
Forrest: The Confederacy's Relentless Warrior
Robert M. Browning, Jr.
Meade: Victor of Gettysburg
Richard A. Sauers
Hindenburg: Icon of German Militarism
William J. Astore/Dennis E. Showalter
Franco: Soldier, Commander, Dictator
Geoffrey Jensen